Praise for *The Magical*

"Using a combination of methods from various traditions and cultures, Elhoim Leafar presents us nothing less than a manual on the magical arts. From magic circles and planetary correspondences to utilizing color associations, herbs, stones, bones, and the phases of the moon, Leafar offers simple methods for the creation and consecration of charm bags for a veritable plethora of practical purposes. Easy to understand and full of interesting details, *The Magical Art of Crafting Charm Bags* is a great guide for the beginner but will also provide the seasoned practitioner with new perspectives on the art of making one of the most beloved forms of spells that folk-magic has to offer."

—Storm Faerywolf, author of *Betwixt and Between: Exploring the Faery Tradition of Witchcraft*

"It is clear when reading *The Magical Art of Crafting Charm Bags* that Elhoim Leafar knows what magick is, namely 'an ancient and noble force capable of generating all kinds of effects in space and time.' He unlocks the keys to this magick providing basic, yet vital, information needed to get started creating altars, talismans, and, ultimately, charm bags. If you are looking for ways to improve and expand your magick this is the book for you."

—Lilith Dorsey, author of *Love Magic*

"*The Magical Art of Crafting Charm Bags* blends multiple cultures into a working system of magical potency. It is a useful grimoire and reference for any magical practitioner. Within its pages, you can learn to put magic in the palm of your hand."

—Adam Sartwell, co-founder of the Temple of Witchcraft and award-winning author of *Twenty-One Days of Reiki* and *The Blessing Cord*

THE Magical Art of Crafting Charm Bags

100 Mystical Formulas for Success, Love, Wealth, and Wellbeing

Elhoim Leafar

Foreword by Devin Hunter

WEISER BOOKS

This edition first published in 2017 by Weiser Books, an imprint of
Red Wheel/Weiser, LLC
With offices at:
65 Parker Street, Suite 7
Newburyport, MA 01950
www.redwheelweiser.com

ISBN: 978-1-57863-619-8

Library of Congress Cataloging-in-Publication Data

Names: Leafar, Elhoim, 1987- author.
Title: The magical art of crafting charm bags : 100 mystical formulas for
    success, love, wealth, and wellbeing / by Elhoim Leafar.
Description: Newburyport : Weiser Books, 2017. | Includes index.
Identifiers: LCCN 2017008986 | ISBN 9781578636198 (5.5 x 8.5 tp : alk.
    paper)
Subjects: LCSH: Witchcraft. | Charms--Miscellanea. | Magic.
Classification: LCC BF1566 .L43 2017 | DDC 133.4/4--dc23
LC record available at https://lccn.loc.gov/2017008986

Cover design by Jim Warner
Cover photograph by David F. Dagnino Viloria
Interior by Deborah Dutton
Typeset in Adobe Garamond Pro, Muriel Regular, and Koch Antiqua

Printed in Canada
MAR

10 9 8 7 6 5 4 3 2 1

Dedication

This book is a tribute to all those who were here before us.

Each time we perform a magic ritual, we use different herbs, crystals, stones, plants, flowers, and oils extracted from Mother Earth to channel various energies. But we must remember that this powerful energy was once in the hands of our ancestors and that, even now, they remain a part of it—a part of its memory, its essence, and its spirit. Thus, through the practice of magic and sorcery, we honor our ancestors. We channel them and embrace them in an eternal cycle of colorful energies that rotates between planes and reaches our hands.

This book is for all those who have discovered the power of magic and inherited the ancestral wisdom that connects us to Mother Earth, to the Sun, to the Moon, and to the rest of the stars in the sky, in all of their various phases. This book is meant to honor them from a small corner of every magic shop and every house where a witch, a sorcerer, a magician, or a believer dwells.

May this book be a balm for your spirit and a fresh breath of magic for your home. May it be a talisman of wisdom and a powerful force for magic in your life, every day of your life. Read it, study it, and let it guide your practice. And may it teach you to become an agent of magic in the lives of those around you. May it guide you on your path to becoming a powerful mage, honoring your ancestors by helping others through its magical lore. May you yourself become a charm bag full of blessings, magic, and wisdom. May you do magic every day and may your days be full of happiness. This is the best gift you can give to your ancestors.

To my ancestors and yours, blessed be their spirits in every life and every cycle, always.

Blessings, Elhoim.

Contents

just being initiated into the practice of the occult arts so they can protect themselves from negative spiritual manifestations.

In traditional magic, the circle serves two primary functions: it protects you from external forces and gives you power for your rituals. The proper performance of an effective spell or ritual always involves the use of an enchanted portal that can be created from different elements. The circle keeps the energy focused at a specific site and allows for the closure of these magical portals at the end of the ritual. It also creates a shield against all kinds of psychic attack and energy loss.

It is common in magic performed in the home to create a magic circle to separate yourself from mystical powers that work with external energies that might somehow alter or interfere with your magical work. After using the circle, you can always erase it. But be sure to close the circle first to dissipate the energy completely. The proper way to close a circle will be explained later in this chapter. After closing the circle, you can sweep it away with a broom, always sweeping from east to west in order not to corrupt the energies and to maintain a perfect balance.

As we say in magic: "All inside the circle; nothing outside the circle." Inside the magic circle, you can perform all sorts of spells, invocations, and rituals. Its magic will keep you protected during these operations and also prevent other individuals who may be present in the house (but not in the same room) from perceiving any change in mood or energy while you are performing your ritual.

You can perform spells and rituals outdoors or in closed sites. When magic is performed outdoors—for instance, in parks or at beaches—it takes on more power by coming into direct contact with Nature and the elements. When performing magic outdoors, we tend to feel less oppressed, and this feeling is transferred to our spells, allowing them to develop more freedom and power.

Magic performed in closed sites has a major disadvantage because the magical energies are obstructed and transmuted, slowing the effective development of the spell. On the other hand, magic

Chapter 1

The Magic Circle

A magic circle is a ritual space created for use as part of a magical work or summoning. It also plays an important role as a link or portal between two planes—the physical and the spiritual. The circle symbolizes greatness, unity, eternity, wisdom, the continuity of the universe, and the infinite cycles of time. It is used to frame a neutral space in which to carry out various spells or rituals. Within that sacred space, you are protected from all kinds of hauntings or negative manifestations.

Every time we perform magic or rituals that somehow work with a different form of energy from our own, we manifest powers of other planes in our world, making invisible portals that remain open for a long time in that place. It is very common for other entities of different planes to take advantage of these portals to move into our world and cause conflict. In magic and sorcery, we perform all kinds of rituals, spells, and incantations inside a magic circle so that their energy will not be altered in any way by external elements.

When you draw a magic circle, this automatically encloses the space and dissolves the energies within it, thus creating a neutral place within which to work. Inside the circle, you can channel and transform energies and use them to create the effect sought by your ritual. Magic circles are especially recommended for those

PART I

The Ancient and Noble Art

Marie Laveau, she knows the truth. She guides her children from beyond the grave.

A gris-gris bag you must craft, red brick powder, pepper and salt, some broken bones and limestones, scent it with oil, do it on the altar. From all vice the gris-gris will protect you.

use of magical qualities. Only you can decide what level of contact you will have with your personal magical ocean, and only you can decide how deeply you will dive into it.

But whatever you decide, that vast and deep ocean is right there at your fingertips.

and your loved ones, enhancing your mental skills and psychic powers, and finally, harnessing the power of the zodiac to take control of your life.

Magic is an ancient and noble force capable of generating all kinds of effects in space and time. It is the power hidden behind each and every force of Nature and the original cause of all the energies that surround us, from our first breath to our last. It existed before Creation, and, when everything ends, it will persist in order to spark creation all over again. Magic is the energetic glue of all causes and effects. It is an integral part of us all—believers and non-believers alike—although it defies all attempts at definition.

Ancient people made use of magic in its various forms to bring rain and calm storms; others used a darker form of it to contact the dead. Today, some use it for divination rites that allow them to predict the future or to reveal the identity of an ideal lover. Magic is a mystical energy that manifests itself in every act, every movement, and every flicker of humanity. It is as massive a force as the oceans. We may never understand it fully, but, as practitioners and students of this ancient art, we are capable of storing a small amount of this energy and using it to our best advantage.

Imagine that you are sitting on the sand in front of a vast ocean, admiring its scope and power. You notice that some use the oceans to sail to distant lands, while others simply use it for swimming, relaxing, or playing. Some may sit beside you on the shore and use the ocean waters to moisten the shapeless sand and turn it into beautiful castles. Yet others may just walk along the shore side by side, testing the water, but not having the courage to venture in. The mystical energy of the universe is similar to the power we perceive in the ocean, although obviously greater.

Our relationship to the ocean is similar to the relationship that many have with magic—an experimental relationship, but also quite a complex one. That relationship may be based on curiosity, grounded in highly academic study, or driven by the real practical

Magic and witchcraft share many common elements. Some are easily recognizable, while others are more obscure, although equally relevant. Among these elements is the creation and use of charm bags, also known as amulet bags, gris-gris bags, and by many other names. Charm bags have commonly been used in various forms of witchcraft, African Diaspora traditions like Voodoo, and shamanism for centuries. The information in this book will help you successfully implement these practices and techniques to suit the needs of *your* life.

Crafting these bags is a practical form of sorcery that uses plants, gems and semi-precious stones, and many other items that are easily found around the home. This manual will show you simple ways to craft charm bags and how to use them in your daily practice. It also provides a guide to magical correspondences for the days of the week, the lunar phases, common garden plants, semi-precious crystals and gems, colors, candles, and more. In fact, you can apply the techniques you find here to any form of magic that you practice. I invite you to master the energies of all the elements around you and use them to improve every aspect of your life.

This book will teach you simple ways to make charm bags for different magical purposes. In part I, we'll start with a brief discussion of some of the important elements of general magical practice—elements that will play a part in our discussion of charm bags. In part II, we'll explore simple methods for crafting charm bags, as well as the proper way to consecrate them. You will also learn the best astrological times for making and using them in order to achieve maximum results. Then you'll learn about a variety of objects that can be used in charm bags and how to empower them using color, time, place, and feeling for the most effective spells and rituals. In part III, you'll find instructions for making charm bags you can use for a wide variety of purposes—achieving abundance and success, ensuring good physical and mental health, attracting love and enriching relationships, invoking protection for yourself

Introduction

When I was eleven, I found a red felt bag stuffed with dried herbs and a bright pebble in the garden of the house where we lived. I took the bag to my mother and she said: "Apparently someone lost their protection. So be it. They will have to build another." She did not question me about this strange talisman, nor did she explain its function or use.

When I was fourteen, a close friend of the family gave me a tiny leather bag and made me promise that I would never open it. She assured me that it was for my protection and said that, if one day I lost it, I should not look for it, because it would have carried away any negative intent that others may have toward me.

At age fifteen, I discovered an old book devoted to esoteric subjects in a small second-hand book shop. Its cover was missing; its pages were wrinkled and translucent with age. The book's author discussed psychic protection, including some unusual handcrafted charm bags containing all kinds of amulets and spells.

Since then, I've spent years studying gypsy magic, Voodoo, and the folkloric and magical traditions of Africa. And now, I think it's time to share some of what I've learned about the tradition and practice of charm bags.

And the witch, in her modernity, did not know the magic that protected the innocent man from all her spells. Hexes, potions, and all sorts of rituals, neither did they seem to affect him, nor did they seem even to get close to him. She did not know this ancient magic that came from the depths of the forest—a bag of leather stuffed with some dried herbs and a few stones, hanging around the neck of the man, who had kept it as a memento of his deceased mother. It was this very amulet in its simplicity that protected the man from all the unknown evils sent by the angry witch.

Acknowledgments

To all who have been part of this magical project.

To David, for your constant support in every aspect, every hour, and every day. There are no words in any language written by man to thank you enough.

To Judika for the opportunity, the trust, the support. For every day, for every phone call, for every piece of advice, and for every message. Where, more than a year ago, I glimpsed only a closed door—hard to open, hidden behind a thick curtain of smoke—you came with a key and a smile saying: "We can, and we will, do it." For all this, thank you hardly seems adequate.

To all the incredible Red Wheel Weiser team. You have done an amazing job overseeing every detail and every aspect of this project, taking my manuscript and turning it into something magical, something worthy, something unique. You are the true alchemists behind this work.

To Devin Hunter, your support is a blessing to those who come only once between many lives; we need more enterprising souls like you to positively change every corner of this world.

To all who contributed to this book—whether of this world or another—profound thanks.

Elhoim has lived the mysteries that he writes about in this book, and it is made clear with every sentence that he is genuinely passionate about the art he practices. This passion spills forth from every page and every charm to create a deep well for us to draw from. One so deep that it fills us up and leaves us feeling as though we have walked in the shoes of a true mystic. Elhoim seems to be tapped into an oneiric truth about magic and the way we interact with it that we are not likely to see again. His is a unique voice, one forged from experience and determination, and he uses that voice to shed light into the depths of a topic that is often overlooked.

As you approach this book, do so with the understanding that you are peering through the lens of a folk practitioner from Venezuela, someone whose methods have been forged through real-life struggle and lifelong training. The magic presented here is part of his unique story as a spiritualist, mystic, and magical practitioner and though flavored with cultural influences from around the world, still finds a way to remain authentic to the regional practices of Elhoim's upbringing. In my opinion, this makes this book a collectable gem worthy of any bookshelf and a go-to for anyone looking for a snapshot of the popular folk practices related to charm bags.

—Devin Hunter, author of *The Witch's Book of Power* and
The Witch's Book of Spirits

perpetual students of the arcane means that we must always be on the search for a different perspective, if only to deepen our own. Magic has this way of always reminding us that we have seen only what we have allowed ourselves to see and that just when we think we know it all there is someone else who knows a thing or two that we don't.

Yes, magic is everywhere, and there are plenty of books on the market that can teach you the steps to harnessing it; but it is rare that a book goes the extra mile and paints a picture of what it is like to experience it. That elusive and all too fleeting "different perspective" that is so important for sage practitioners can be gained only when a book showcases the experience surrounding the subject, helping the reader navigate that practice for themselves. The benefit to us as the reader is that when an author can do this we are given the advantage of intuiting what we are *supposed* to sense when we perform the magic for ourselves.

Rare indeed that a book is able to approach a topic in this way, because it requires its author to be completely authentic, to know their muse inside and out, and to perhaps even bare a bit of their soul in the process of writing. There must be a personal and direct approach that yields not only mental insight but that allows the reader to feel as though they are receiving wisdom that was harvested through experience.

Within these pages, you will find answers to questions you didn't know you had, spells and charms that you will want to add to your arsenal, and plenty of inspiration for the path to come. Guided by the mind of a highly skilled mystic, this book reads as both a manual and a testament for the magic of charm bags. Be it Elhoim's Consecration ritual which teaches you to harness your emotions in order to fuel your spell or one of his many charm bag recipes for success, money, or protection, there is little that goes uncovered.

tion to detail that is taken when making it, not to mention the discipline surrounding its upkeep.

Magic is a force that exists all around us. It is in the air we breathe, the water we drink, the ground we walk upon, and, for many of us, the blood in our veins. Practicing a magical tradition such as Witchcraft, Conjure, Vodou, or Folk Magic allows us to tap into this force and use it for ourselves. Throughout each of these traditions there are practices that can be found to exist in tandem; the charm bag being one of the most common and cherished among them.

Perhaps the practice of creating charm bags comes from our animal instinct to collect and carry items of value, protecting them at all costs. Perhaps it derives from the animistic and sympathetic world views these traditions tend to have, knowing that different ingredients have the power to influence the forces of magic and bend its flow to obtain a desired result. No matter its root, the practice is one that can be found in almost every single magical tradition and can be traced to every shore.

Charm bags come in all shapes and sizes and go by many different names; putsi, gris-gris, mojo, medicine bag, and sorcerer's hand to name a few. They are by far one of the most versatile and useful forms of talismans available and are relatively simple to make. However, like most magic, simplicity and familiarity can often be confused for inefficiency or lack of imagination, making this form of magic among the most underestimated in the esoteric toolbox.

For many of us, the topic and praxis related to charm bags was presented by someone who had only a superficial understanding of the subject, leaving the pupil no wiser. The vast majority of us, however, have never had the privilege of a teacher and rely on books for the bulk of our training, and because the subject of charm bags is only lightly breached in popular tomes, there is much to be desired and plenty of questions surrounding the topic. Luckily, being worked with them for so long that I am convinced that they possess their own personalities. Always willing to express gratitude for an offering well-made and always willing to express disappointment when I have lacked on my end of the bargain. Faithful to me and me alone, these charm bags are crafted from the finest ingredients and, in some cases, took months to make. Raw opals from Australia, volcanic ash from Mt. St. Helens, a feather gifted by an owl-keeper, and the dried husks of an Amazonian pitcher-plant are some of the curios you might find among my wares. Each article was carefully selected and laboriously nurtured, before combining it with the others. Every magical practitioner has their own special way of constructing charm bags and no two are quite the same, our secret alterations kept close to the heart.

While visiting New Orleans, Salem, and San Francisco, a favorite activity of mine is to visit the various magic shops and take a look at their offerings. You can get charm bags over the counter or you can talk to someone, and, in some shops, they will even make you one right on the spot, for a small fee of course. Aside from those rare handmade charm bags found in those special shops that are crafted just for you, it is actually quite difficult to find a quality charm bag for sale. Typically, the ones on the market are mass produced, and, if you're lucky, they have been prayed over once before being packaged and shipped. Their value derives only from the ease in which they can be procured, rather than their actual magical inheritance.

Not surprisingly, my most prized charm bag is made of the simplest ingredients. Anointed prayer-paper talismans and herbs stuffed into a swatch of fabric that was ripped from an old shirt. It lives in a special box on a special altar and has never been seen by anyone but me. It isn't the extraordinary ingredients that make a charm bag powerful nor the city of its origin, but rather the atten-

Foreword

"By my mind and my body, by my soul and my will,
I conjure a magic that's focused and still

By curio and herb, by darkness and light,
I conjure a talisman with strength and with might.

By breath and by smoke, by oil and key
I conjure a charm that's tied just to me.

By blessings and prayers, by songs and by rhyme
I conjure a spirit that will grow in time.

With this enchantment, my sovereign decree,
I conjure my ally, so shall it be!"

—The Conjuring of the Charm Bag,
from my own Book of Shadows.

Currently I have a charm bag in every room of my house and business, in my car, as well as two that travel with me on my many adventures. I consider them to be trusty companions along the all too often lonely road of life. Some of them are so old and I have done indoors has the advantage of conveying calm and privacy—important factors today, considering how crowded many outdoor spaces have become with children playing, runners, smokers, and many other sources of loud noises.

European folklore prescribes a magic circle drawn with salt to ward off headaches resulting from psychic attack or spells. Spanish and British lore calls for a circle of salt under the dining table to prevent diseases and food poisoning. In many traditions, salt is a purifying element that prevents evil and wards off bad luck. According to the mystical legends of Avalon, witches who dedicated themselves to evil and ghosts who sought to do harm could not step on salt or pass through an area blessed with it. Because of this, perhaps the most common kind of magic circle is one drawn on the floor in a clockwise direction using coarse or rock salt, or even common table salt.

The circle can also be "drawn" with elements of protection like a cord or rope, or a ribbon blessed on St. John's Eve. In white magic, it is common to draw circles under the bed with ropes or salt to avoid having your sleep disturbed by negative entities that commonly move at night. All these versions of the magic circle have protective qualities. Salt and rosemary are recognized in white magic, along with garlic and vervain, as elements of powerful protection against evil, malicious hauntings, and spirits. A line of salt in door frames and windows, for instance, protects you from people with bad intentions.

Some practitioners add pieces of quartz to their circles to create a more effective and powerful space. To do this, collect pieces of quartz and consecrate them on a Monday night by anointing them with essential oil of rosemary and verbena. Save them in a silver or purple bag like one you would use for an amulet. Before performing a magical ritual, make your circle as usual and place the consecrated quartz crystals as part of the circle to charge it with their protective energies. When you are finished, return the crystals to their pouch for use in future rituals. In chapter 9, you will find a list of crystals that lend themselves to magic circles, along with information on their various properties.

Casting a Magic Circle

To create a magic circle, choose a site for your ritual and draw a circle four to six feet in diameter on the floor. The circle must always be traced by a single person and always in a clockwise direction. Magic circles are usually drawn using chalk or salt, as the color white symbolizes the absolute power of purification. You can also use sea salt and a mixture of protective herbs like rosemary and melissa to ward off negative energies and evil spirits that may be involved in your ritual.

Rope Circles

Another common version of the magic circle is one "drawn" with magic rope. Consecrate the rope to charge it with the magical power of protection on your personal altar with a mixture of oils and herbs on a St. John's night. Keep the consecrated rope under your altar as a means of protection. When you are ready to perform a ritual, shape it into a circle on the floor to create a space that will channel and focus the mystical energies required for your work. Make sure your ceremonial circle is large enough to accommodate all aspects of your ritual.

The Full Moon, Samhain, or Walpurgis night are the best times for consecrating your rope. Once consecrated, roll up the rope and bury it in a yard or garden at a shallow depth, or place it in a large pot and cover it with soil and some poppy seeds or fruit peels to symbolize the forest and its mystical energy. The rope must remain buried at least until the next night, when you can dig it up and "show it to the Moon" for a few minutes, as if presenting it to the spiritual world. A rope buried on the Full Moon and released the next night symbolizes rebirth, reincarnation, and all the cycles of life and death.

Keeping a consecrated rope on hand as a practical, fully charged ceremonial tool can save you time when performing your rituals. For many practitioners of various forms of magic, creating a circle of protection may seem tedious, as it involves laying the circle and then closing it and sweeping it away. These practitioners often prefer to use a consecrated rope because they can simply retrieve the rope from their altars, lay the circle, and then return it to its place once their ceremonies are complete.

Consecrating a Magic Rope

You can consecrate your magic rope on your personal altar, or in a small garden nearby if you want to channel energies from Mother Earth more effectively. Start with a thick rope at least six feet (two meters) long. Make a preparation with water from a nearby river or spring—avoid bottled water and only use tap water as a last resort. Combine the water with essential oils for protection and blessing, like rosemary, sandalwood, eucalyptus, or vervain. In chapter 10, you will find a list of essential aromatic oils that can be used for this consecration and blessing.

Anoint the rope from one end to the other with your magical mix, channeling your positive thoughts, your desire for protection, and your best energies into it. Focus on the rope for a few moments to make it a barrier of energetic protection for all of your rituals. Keep your consecrated rope in a sack or bag of dark fabric. You can anoint it with a few drops of aromatic herbal oil each Full Moon at midnight, just as the spirits and deities walk among us, in order to keep it positively charged.

Herbal Circles

Herbal mixtures are also widely used today to draw magic circles. These mixtures usually consist of dried herbs of protection, like rosemary, sage, vervain, garlic, and orange flower. Mix and crush the herbs together and save them in a bottle. Each time you perform a magical operation or work, draw a circle on the floor with the herbal mix you prepared. You can also store your herbal mix in a little bag of green cloth and perfume it with a few drops of essential oil of peppermint, vervain, and sandalwood to create an amulet you can wear to protect yourself from all evil.

Consecrating Magic Herbs

On the night prior to the Full Moon, fill a pot or large vase with equal parts of mint, sea salt, rosemary, verbena, apple, and sage. Crush the herbs and mix them together, then add a few drops of essential oil of geranium and verbena. Let the mixture sit overnight by the window under the light of the Full Moon. The next morning, transfer your blend of consecrated herbs to a covered jar and keep it sealed in a cool area. You can periodically make more of this mix using the same herbs and add it to the jar. You can use this consecrated mix to replace salt or white chalk to create a magic circle full of herbal energies that will give your rituals the blessing of the Earth and the increased energy of the most powerful phase of the Moon.

Closing the Magic Circle

There are several methods to close a magic circle. Which one you use will depend on the type of circle you have made. Be careful when choosing, however, because closing the circle in the wrong way can easily spoil the magic work that has been done.

It is important to close a magic circle when your ritual is finished, because it can act as a portal between worlds that various spirits and diverse souls can use to pass between the physical and spiritual planes. Your circle of power is literally a metaphysical elevator that allows you to move to other planes of existence and extract from them what is necessary to make your ritual effective—spirits to consult on some matter, extra energies to strengthen your spell, forces to empower an object or talisman, or even ethereal knowledge from ascended masters and higher spirits.

As you close your magic circle, I suggest thanking those who have accompanied you during the ritual, whether alive or dead. Whether you have performed the ritual in a group or with the deities and spirits of your own pantheon, it is always best to give thanks for any help you may have received. If you have invoked any particular spirits or divinities, thank them by placing a glass of water, incense, and scented candles on your altar. Once you have given thanks, you can close the circle.

To close the circle, start with a brief magical prayer. This can be something simple, like:

Thanks to all those present during the ritual.
The magic is done correctly today and always.
Blessed be tomorrow and always.
May the circle be closed until it is necessary to open it again.

Or:

The magic work has ended.
The circle has closed.
The magic for today has ended.

If you wish, you can also develop your own magic spell or phrase to close the circle. If you do, memorize it and pronounce it many times in front of a mirror to give it greater power.

If the circle was made with powder—talcum powder, salt, sugar, or herbs—you can close it by sweeping with a broom from east to west to dissipate any remaining energy. If, on the other hand, the circle was made with an enchanted rope, retrieve the rope from the ground with both hands and store it in a large bag previously anointed with herbal oils to maintain its properties. If the circle was made with flower petals, collect them and store them in a large jar. Then bury the jar at the foot of a tree. To close a circle made entirely of consecrated crystals, collect the crystals one by one, moving in a clockwise direction, and place them in a large bowl of cold water mixed with sea salt. Let them remain there for several hours, or even a whole night, to purify them.

To close a circle cast with herbs and flowers, use a bowl of water that you have blessed in advance with a few drops of essential oil of vervain, mint, or cascara. Sprinkle the water over the circle, moving in a clockwise direction—first from one end to the other, and then from the inside to the outside.

In Santería and Candomble, as well as in other esoteric traditions linked to Afro-Caribbean spiritism, it is customary to close circles by sealing them with rose water or the popular "florida water," which can be found in esoteric shops. According to popular belief, this calms the spirits and dissipates the energies.

Some more recent traditions, like Wicca, use "Moon water" to close the circle. This consists of fresh water mixed with pieces of quartz that has been exposed to moonlight for a full night before the day of the ritual, then placed in a sealed container inside the magic circle. When the ritual is finished, the Moon water is poured onto four points in the circle, symbolizing lunar rain that seals the four cardinal points from which the energy emanates.

Whichever method you choose to close your circle, always remember to light an incense stick in the center of the place where the circle was positioned. You can also include a white candle to balance any energies that may remain. Lighting a white candle at each end of the room near the corners can also help to cleanse the space and repel any residual energy.

As a very traditional spiritist, I also recommend that you prepare a small bundle of herbs known as a *sahumerio*. To do this, take peppermint, mint, parsley, and a couple of chrysanthemum flowers and bind them tightly with white, red, and black ribbons (the colors of God Eleggua, the Road Opener). Anoint the bundle with rose oil or rose water and use it like a small broom to cleanse every corner and surface of the room where a magic ritual has been performed.

Chapter 2

The Altar and the Pentagram

Like the magic circle, the altar and the pentagram are elements common to most magical traditions—elements that will play a role in our discussion of charm bags in chapters to come. Altars usually consist of a small table or other piece of furniture covered with a cloth or a colorful scarf on which you place objects and symbols associated with your personal faith—candles, an incense burner, magical tools, objects of divination, and any other items appropriate to your practice. The pentagram is a magical symbol so ancient that its true origin remains unknown. It is a symbol that has always been linked to folklore, mysticism, and magic in all its incarnations, from traditional paganism to modern Wicca.

The Altar

Although most spiritual and magical traditions use altars in their practice, these altars take many different forms. Spiritualist altars usually contain glasses of water representing life, candles symbolizing energy, and photographs and images of ancestors or deities. Some include a large mirror to reflect the mage during rituals, as well as candles of different colors and shapes, and images corresponding to the deities in his or her pantheon. For practitioners of Wicca and other forms of white magic, altars usually incorporate representations of the four elements of Nature: candles to symbolize Fire, a censer to represent Air, a saucer or pot of salt or sand to symbolize Earth, and a glass or cup of water to represent the element of life. In Afro-Brazilian folklore, altars are usually filled with aromatic and medicinal herbs, images of clay symbolizing the sorcerer or priest, bells to honor the spirits and deities of the Yoruba pantheon, fans, ethnic ornaments, and white candles. On the other hand, a traditional Voodoo altar usually contains representations of the four elements; herbs; aromatic flowers; candles to honor the dead and familiar spirits; ornaments made from bones, skin, and colored feathers; and different oracular and divination tools.

In almost all magical traditions, however, the altar is seen as a sacred place from which practitioners conduct their respective magical operations. I see the altar, not as a religious shrine, but rather as a place of personal power—a place where you can freely express your beliefs and practice the teachings of your particular brand of spirituality. Your personal altar is a portal that connects you to the other side—a mystical space where you can perform your magical work successfully. It is a place that allows you to get in touch with the gods and higher spirits—a focal point for meditation, visualization, and, in some cases, divination.

Although some esoteric traditions give very precise instructions on how to organize an altar and tend to it, I think the most important factor to consider when creating your personal altar is to make sure that the site is comfortable for you, that it is practical for your work, and that it is a reflection of your own beliefs. Choose an area of the house where you feel comfortable—preferably the main room or an illuminated area opposite the main door. If you have a garden with a covered area, you can place your personal altar there, or you can place it in a small corner of a room that is blessed with natural light and fresh breezes. This option is often preferred by those who share a house with someone who does not share their beliefs.

Your altar should represent you as its owner and keeper. Add candles of different colors and sizes, but always include a white candle to honor your ancestors, your deceased loved ones, and all those who have gone on before you but are still looking out for you. Include a censer to perfume and purify the ritual space, symbols or emblems of protection, sachets filled with dried herbs, aromatic flowers, and religious images representing the faith you follow. It is always advisable to include at least one glass or cup of water for the spirits and deities.

Some people decorate their altars with gems and various colored minerals to balance the magical energies in their favor. Others prefer to include flowers from their gardens or herbs from a nearby park to channel Earth energies. Yet others place pictures of deceased loved ones and ancestors on their altars to honor them and commune with them every day.

Keep all the elements and tools you use during magical operations near your altar—matches, books and reference manuals, incense, needle and thread, pen and paper, and everything you may need to support your rituals. Keep a calendar nearby so you can check lunar phases, astrological signs, and the energy processes that govern daily life. These factors can complement and empower your work, and you can learn a little more about them in the process.

It is very important to keep your altar clean, tidy, and organized all the time. Don't just tend to it when you are going to perform a ritual or magical operation. Perfume it regularly with dried herbs or aromatic oils to keep those who hear your pleas and magical prayers happy and close to you.

The Pentagram

The pentagram is a mystical symbol in the form of a five-pointed star within a circle. Today, it is easy to find pentagrams of all materials, colors, and sizes in esoteric shops and specialty catalogs, or worn as decorative jewelry or talismans. In fact, I'm sure you've all seen pentagrams at one time or another on the covers of books, on television, on posters, or in the movies.

In ancient times, witches made use of the pentagram to ward off evil and evil spirits. They also used it to conjure up the forces of Nature and carry out different types of spells and rituals linked to them, or to channel the energies of the natural world. A pentagram recently found in the Tigris-Euphrates valley is said to represent the astronomical passage of Venus, which has a total of five conjunctions with the Sun and Earth every eight years. Another, dating back to 3500 B.C.E., symbolized the enormous power that the ruler of Mesopotamia had over the nation. In fact, pentagrams are often used to represent imperial power in pottery, architecture, and handicrafts, on stamps, and as part of royal inscriptions.

According to a variety of esoteric and religious traditions, the four lower points of the pentagram symbolize the four elements of Nature—Fire, Air, Earth, and Water. For many followers of the Kabbalistic or Hindu traditions, the upper tip symbolizes the "ether" or spirit, while for practitioners of modern magic, it is often associated with the mind of man, which can master the four elements of Nature. In modern magic, the circle enclosing the star is the "ether" or spirit, which contains everything within itself. For Hebrews, the pentagram is a symbol of divine truth and also represents the five books of the Pentateuch. In the Eastern tradition of *feng shui*, it represents the five elements that protect the secrets of the universe—fire, water, earth, wood, and metal. In Venezuela and Argentina, iron pentagrams are buried near rivers and forests where witches and sorcerers gather to perform their rituals to strengthen their magical energies.

The pentagram symbolizes the human mind taking control over the elements of Nature. Drawing a pentagram on any surface is commonly thought to bring good luck, while drawing or hanging a pentagram on a door is said to keep away unwanted guests and discourage visitors with bad intentions. Hanging a talisman containing a pentagram from a baby crib wards off the Evil Eye and all kinds of spirits that have dark intentions toward the child. A tattoo in the form of a pentagram is said to keep you free from curses and hexes. A ring, bracelet, necklace, or other piece of jewelry with a pentagram on it has the power to strengthen all kinds of spells and rituals by creating a perfect balance in the energies. Giving a pentagram to others gives them the power to regain control of their lives and reach equilibrium.

You should always have a pentagram somewhere in your home to bring good luck and drive away evil and all kinds of conflict. You can strengthen your rituals and your spontaneous contact with the "beyond" by simply placing a pentagram on your altar and consecrating it on the night of a Full Moon with a few drops of aromatic herbal oil of your choice. This will bring balance and good fortune to your workings. Today, you can purchase tablecloths and carpets with the symbol of the pentagram on them. Even though these may seem to be purely decorative, the symbol itself is potent, so placing one of these items on or near your altar will better channel the elemental energies.

Pentagrams are always welcome additions to any charm bag, and they can strengthen any talisman you make and increase its effectiveness. Buy tiny pentagrams and add them to your charm bags when you consecrate them. Or, to save money, you can also draw a pentagram on a piece of parchment, paper, or cloth and add it to a charm bag. Either way, it is sure to be beneficial.

Pentagrams are essential in magic, so always have one with you.

Chapter 3

Enchanted Objects

Enchanted objects are items that have been given magical powers through a spell or a ritual. They are important to us here because they are often used in charm bags. In fact, the specific power of any charm bag is dependent on the enchanted objects it contains and the specific enchantments used to consecrate the bag. Indeed, to master the art of crafting charm bags is to master the art of enchantment.

Many people use the terms "talisman" and "amulet" interchangeably. But these are, in fact, different magical objects. An amulet can be any object to which we have given a significant meaning or power—a rabbit's foot, a four-leaf clover, a lucky penny, or a photo of a loved one in a wallet. A talisman, while also an object with magical properties, is a more complicated affair, because its powers or properties come, not only from our belief in them, but also from a ritual called enchantment. A talisman is a unique object; it is personal and nontransferable. It is empowered for a specific use by a series of energetic vibrations that turn it into a powerful tool in both traditional and modern witchcraft. So all talismans are amulets; but not all amulets are talismans.

Enchantments are more complicated than regular spells specifically because they have to be powerful enough to last through time. For this reason, they often rely on astrological associations and energies for their effectiveness. Thus studying astrological charts and lunar calendars is very important to crafting and consecrating effective charm bags.

An enchantment properly consists of charging a magical object with a long-term spell, cosmically linking the object to a particular effect. A spell, on the other hand, is a ritual that generates a magical or ethereal effect that, in turn, generates a physical manifestation—like better health or an improved love life. Spells usually last for short periods; in time, they lose their power and need to be recharged.

Enchantments are performed to link or tie a spell directly to a specific object—essentially, they are the white magic equivalent of a hex or a curse. When enchanting an object, the magical process remains the same. But instead of being simple rituals that are repeated again and again, enchantments tend to be unique and personalized. Because of this, we usually develop our own enchantments, but always by performing the same basic steps: drawing a magic circle, invoking the avatars of the four cardinal points, and then blessing the object.

A charm bag's magic is powered by the practitioner's own personal energy, hence it is permanently linked to the creator of the enchanted objects it contains. Because these objects are powered by their creator's life energy, their effectiveness is linked to the faculties of the mage or sorcerer who made them. The greater the power and experience of the mage, the greater the power and effectiveness of the object. Due to the energy required to enchant an object, I always recommend that you first perform a meditation and enjoy a purifying bath with natural oils to stimulate and strengthen your aura so you aren't exhausted after performing the spell.

In this chapter, we'll look at some traditional enchantments. But remember that you need to practice and experiment to develop your own more creative ones. Those you make yourself will always be more effective than what you can find in a book, because you are the only one who knows how best to channel your own energy and your personal magic to achieve a goal.

A Witch's Talisman

The most powerful object a wise mage or witch can make is his or her own talisman, which will have a special bond with and be linked to the powers of its creator. A witch's personal talisman not only represents its creator; it is also a source of extra power that will support any of the witch's future spells. It is also a gateway through which the witch can access the spiritual plane.

The most important part of creating your own witch's talisman is choosing the right small object to use. First, it has to represent *you*. It should be something you can carry around with you almost all the time—at least while you are charging it—so it must be easy to transport and should not be delicate or fragile. It can be a bag filled with dried herbs and flowers, or you can fill a nicely patterned cloth bag with elements that represent you. You can also craft an object from wood, metal, stones, or crystals—in fact, from just about anything, as long as you inject love and dedication into it. There are no better talismans than those made with your own hands.

If you cannot craft your own talisman, you can buy one in a store or have one custom made. Some people like to use shapes or symbols they believe represent them or that they have always found attractive—a star, the Moon, the Sun, a flower, a pentacle, a pyramid, an animal shape, a decorative shape, writing, or Eastern symbols. Some prefer to carry a gem with their zodiac sign incised on it. There are all kinds of talismans, and your only limitations are those you put on your own creativity.

Once you have chosen or crafted your talisman, it must remain close to you for at least a few weeks for the spell to begin the bonding process. You can wear it as a pin, a necklace, or a bracelet, or carry it in your purse, briefcase, or wallet. You can even carry it around in your pocket. Try not to expose it too much to the view of others, and be sure that others don't touch it. The object is going through a bonding process and any extraneous touch can taint the connection you want to establish between the object and your soul. You want to avoid receiving the energies of others unless they are people you trust or people who are practitioners of white magic themselves. Rather than tainting a talisman, fellow mages may actually strengthen the bonding process by bringing their own best wishes and good vibes to it.

When you are ready to perform your enchantment ritual, be sure to choose a time when you will not be interrupted, preferably during a Crescent Moon. The best possible time is when the Crescent Moon is transiting your own zodiac sign. Prepare your altar and place on it everything you will need for the ritual—a large white candle, incense sticks and an incense cone, a cauldron or a bowl (preferably metal) big enough to hold the talisman and herbs, a new and sterilized needle (preferably from a syringe), a white quartz crystal, a stone from a nearby river or from the sea, ground cinnamon, rock or sea salt, a white cloth or handkerchief, a clean wine glass, enough essential oil of eucalyptus or musk oil to fill the glass, and a preparation of at least three of the following plant roots and leaves: mandrake, rosemary, bay, hawthorn, elder, sage, and apple tree. And don't forget the object you want to enchant.

Before the ceremony, take a purifying bath with scented oils and the natural essences you consider necessary to strengthen your magic and put your mind at peace. You can also use bath salts. Dress in comfortable clothes in positive colors (see chapter 7).

Light a stick of incense in every corner of the house and a cone of incense under your altar. Just before starting the ceremony, prepare a cup of tea made with chamomile leaves, and add mint and rosemary leaves. Leave the tea in the teapot until after the ritual, then drink it to renew your energies.

Charging Your Witch's Talisman

Draw a magic circle around yourself and your altar. Invoke the elemental spirits using the consecration ceremony given in chapter 6. Place your talisman in the bowl or cauldron and completely cover it with the prepared herbal blend. Sprinkle the cinnamon and sea salt on top for protection and extra purification. Add the quartz crystal and the stone. Then prick your finger with the needle and add a few drops of your own blood and, if possible, add a bit of your own sweat. After all of this is complete, light the white candle.

Meditate for about twenty minutes. Visualize your magical power emanating from your body and completely embracing the talisman. Feel your magical power storing itself inside of it. Invoke the blessing of all the great spirits and gods in your pantheon and pour a bit of the white candle's melted wax over the bowl and the mixture. When you are done, lift the talisman from the bottom of the bowl using one hand and place it in the glass. Then fill the glass to the top with eucalyptus or musk oil and cover it with the white cloth. Finally, close your magic circle and cleanse your ritual space. Leave the glass containing your talisman covered until the next Full Moon.

On the next Full Moon, light a stick of jasmine or mint incense and a white candle. Remove the white cloth and retrieve your talisman from the glass. Place it somewhere on your body immediately without letting it dry, because the essential oils that have remained covered for several days are now blessed for your welfare, health, and protection.

Keep your talisman with you until the next Full Moon. Remove it when you bathe or shower, and sleep with it under your pillow. This personal talisman is now linked to you and will ward off accidents and bad omens as long as you keep it close.

Recharging a Talisman

Like any other enchanted object, personal talismans can lose their power over time. It is a good practice to recharge them after the first year of use. The following is a simple ritual you can perform that comes from an old gypsy tradition.

After creating a magic circle, place a blue cloth on your altar, then light some incense and three candles forming a triangle. If possible, use candles that are the same color as your talisman or a color with similar purposes (see chapter 7). Fill a wine glass with water and rock salt to activate the ritual space. Take the talisman in both your hands and slowly pass it seven times clockwise through the incense smoke, which represents the element Air. Then pass it seven times clockwise around the triangle formed by the candles, which represent Fire. Sprinkle the talisman seven times with water from the glass, reciting the following incantation with each pass and sprinkle:

Great avatars in this distant time

Guardian Gods and Godesses, I call upon Thee.

Great Spirits of the North, East, West, and South,

Be with Thee the divine grace of Universal Sooth

And be with me the blessing of the heavens,

Your presence, and your continued favor.

Blessed be all present spirits and gods,

Blessed be all the talismans

Present here in this space.

Finally, leave the talisman in the center of the triangle formed by the candles, or next to it, and bless its power with your mental energies. Remember that your life and mental energy form the primary energies of magic and that they now empower the talisman.

Canceling a Talisman's Power

It is very important to cancel an enchantment when your talisman has served its purpose, because the magic effect will continue to act upon you until you do so. Nor can you give a talisman away after using it because it will continue to act upon you from afar. Moreover, if your talisman falls into malicious hands, it could be used to harm you. When the effect of your personal talisman is no longer useful to you, or you want for any reason to cancel its powers, you must "unenchant it" to eliminate its remaining magic. And since you are the one who created the talisman, you must be the one to cancel its powers.

Canceling a talisman's power is easier than creating it in the first place. Just place it in a bowl filled with sea salt and draw a pentagram with stones around the bowl. Place one black candle in each of the five tips of the pentagram's star. Light them in counterclockwise direction while visualizing how the flames consume the powers of the talisman. Finally, cover the talisman with two spoons of dirt. The candles' flames will consume the talisman's magic, just as they consume the wax of the candles. When the candles have burned down completely and the last candle flame is out, bury the talisman in a flower pot or in a garden to symbolize the return of its powers to Mother Earth.

Chapter 4

Incense

Incense is an aromatic blend of different common plant resins that releases a pleasant fragrance when burned. Incense is usually burned in enclosed spaces for religious or therapeutic purposes. It is commonly used in various mystical or spiritual ceremonies, as well as for aromatherapy and meditation.

Since ancient times, the ceremonial burning of incense has been linked to spirituality and the worship of gods, the rising of its aromatic smoke symbolically representing the prayers of believers ascending to heaven. Incense bears an ideological connection to the Air element as a "messenger being" of the spiritual plane, and its different fragrances are thought to channel or express specific emotions and energies around us.

In modern witchcraft, incense is most commonly used in two of its multiple forms—sticks and cones. Incense sticks are perhaps the most common and best-known form because they are easy to handle. Incense sticks are often used to cleanse homes and to scent rooms and offices, or to "spiritually cleanse" spaces. Incense cones, on the other hand, represent the firmness of the Earth and perseverance. Cones, although perhaps less common, are recommended for burning on personal altars and during spiritual and magical rituals, where they help to keep the mind focused and prevent practitioners from losing their concentration on their goals.

Incense is often used as a fundamental part of rituals linked to paganism and witchcraft. According to folklore, it helps to create a clean and pure atmosphere for conjuring all kinds of energies or invoking various elemental spirits that come forth to receive the fragrant smoke. In addition, since incense is made of aromatic plant resins and natural essences, burning it helps release the energies that are accumulated therein, encouraging an energetically strong atmosphere for performing various rituals and incantations.

Burning incense—whether as sticks, cones, granules, spirals, or solid bars—purifies the atmosphere around you, creating a positive devotional and balanced environment. It strengthens spirituality, attracts different energies according to its fragrance, facilitates the spiritual cleansing of both people and objects, nullifies negative energies, wards off evil spirits, and powers all forms of magic.

The daily practice of burning incense stimulates concentration, increases positive attitudes, and elevates us spiritually, allowing us to achieve a greater degree of awareness about everything around us. Incense can be used to develop psychic abilities through constant meditation. It strengthens the psyche and encourages clairvoyance, while it relaxes the mind and dispels concerns. It is commonly used to purify environments and cleanse them of negative entities and bad influences, as well as to balance positive energies and moods.

In ancient Egypt, incense was burned in temples because its fragrant and soothing smoke enabled the souls of the pharaohs to ascend to the world of the gods without any disturbance. It was also used to invoke the spirits of the dead and the deities who cared for the funerary temples. In ancient Rome, incense was used in ritual sacrifices to the gods, while in shamanic traditions, aromatic incense acted as a mirror or portal that revealed the past and allowed worshippers to contact the spiritual realm and their ancestors. On a more practical note, burning incense at night promotes personal energy and disperses nightmares, while incense burned during the day embues us with good energies and protects us from bad influences. In South America, there is a popular saying: "A house where incense burns by day is home to the great spirits. In a house where incense burns by night, witches do not sleep."

The world of incense is very complex. It includes sedative fragrances like orange blossom and lavender, aphrodisiac fragrances like almond, cinnamon, or vanilla, stimulant fragrances like bergamot and jasmine, and revitalizing fragrances like mint and vetiver. As you will see in chapter 10, all of these magical properties make incense useful in the crafting of charm bags.

PART II

Charm Bags in Tradition and Practice

Every Monday night, the witch visited the cemetery, collecting soil and dried herbs that grew around the graves. She returned home following the path that marked the Moon, filling her gris-gris bag with thirteen elements—owl bones, grave dust, graveyard dirt, red brick dust, white pepper and black pepper, rock salt, wax from a black candle, and dried root of cascara. She added four elements provided by the night—one by Air, one by Fire, one by Water, and one last element offered by the forest. She conjured the souls of her deceased on an altar of olive wood and, before the dark night ended, her personal talisman was made, embroidered on each side with her initials, M. L. And the next morning, she laid to rest all the evils that had been forgotten.

Chapter 5

What Is a Charm Bag?

A charm bag is a magical tool that is either carried as a talisman or used in some other fashion in magical ceremonies. It consists of a small bag or pouch that contains a cohesive and vibrationally harmonious group of enchanted objects. Charm bags are used to attract, strengthen, weaken, cancel, or dissipate different magical effects through regular contact with them. Mages usually make their own charm bags, but they can also be made to benefit someone else. They are very popular among modern witches, Neopagans, shamans, and those who practice various forms of spiritualism, Voodoo, Hoodoo, and other African Diaspora traditions.

Charm bags offer a practical and yet simple way to carry your spells with you. They are meant to be worn daily, and can be hung around the neck or carried in a personal bag, purse, pocket, or backpack. Typically, they are made from felt or flannel cloth, although other fabrics can be used. They may be filled with a single type of ingredient, like magic herbs, or they may be filled with diverse and varied ingredients—for instance, a combination of herbs, bones, stones, and small images or magical figures. For example, a charm bag intended to ward off envy and jealousy may contain herbs and gems that possess protective qualities, like rosemary, garlic, and garnet, or even a tiny piece of mirror to reflect evil back to its source. On the other hand, a charm bag intended to strengthen clairvoyance during divination may be crafted using artemisia, geranium, and camphor.

Moreover, you can craft charm bags for your friends and loved ones. And you can learn a lot about the different aspects of magic and its natural energies in the process, because making them puts you in direct contact with elements of Nature like stones and plants that have different magical properties.

With a charm bag, you can perform simple but effective magic that does not require assistance from other individuals or complicated invocations of spirits that you may, at times, prefer to avoid—whether because of inexperience, fear of the unknown, or lack of knowledge. When you carry a charm bag, you harmonize with its mystical energy. Constant contact with it helps you to channel the bag's magical effects, unlike spells and magic formulas that can seem ethereal or merely theoretical, or that seem to lack practical or concrete results.

Charm Bags in Magical Tradition

The use of charm bags is quite common in the gypsy culture, where women are renowned for their great healing and protective powers. gypsy charm bags are similar in form and use in several respects to those made by practitioners of modern witchcraft. For example, they both rely on the natural energies of herbs and medicinal plants to produce a wide range of effects, and they both include symbolic elements—for example, coins in bags intended to bring good luck and fortune.

Another popular type of charm bag is known as a "gris-gris" bag. Gris-gris bags are common in New Orleans because of their associations with Marie Laveau, the Queen of Voodoo, who is perhaps the one most famous for using this particular form of magic.

Gris-gris bags are specifically made to provide mystical or spiritual protection to the individuals who carry them. They ward off bad luck, bad influences, the Evil Eye, and malicious spirits. Charm bags intended for any purpose other than protection are known as "spell containers" throughout Europe and South America. In Venezuela, my home country, they are colloquially known as "bags of blessings." These are made in the Santería tradition using dried herbs, river stones, spices, graveyard dirt, coarse salt, and pepper, all deposited in a tiny bag of dark fabric and dedicated to African, Brazilian, and Afro-Cuban deities.

Today, gris-gris bags have become souvenirs for tourists, but they are also prepared by experienced witches or priestesses using various forms of witchcraft that combine elements of traditional magic, Voodoo, and spiritualism. In West Africa, Tuareg nomads craft gris-gris bags from leather and fill them with bones, stones, amulets, feathers, strands of hair, and ashes to ward off evil spirits and disease. Travelers passing through the Gulf of Guinea were given gifts of gris-gris bags made by a shaman or local priest to protect them from disease and the demons of the desert. During the dark days of slavery, those brought from Africa often carried treasured gris-gris bags around their necks, charged with a shaman's blessings of protection. Because of this and the more positive diffusion of African culture in recent decades, gris-gris bags are powerful components of various currents of African Diaspora spiritual traditions like Voodoo and Hoodoo (or Conjure), as well as other streams of African spirituality like Santería, Candomble, Macumba, Umbanda, and Quimbanda. These African traditions exerted a strong influence on American culture by combining their folkloric magic with the more religious European tradition of magic, resulting in the Voodoo dolls, gris-gris bags, and hanging talismans (necklaces and pendants) that have become so popular today.

Crafting Charm Bags

Charm bags are a complex form of very ancient magic, and their various elements and ingredients require a lot of study. Before starting to craft charm bags, you must be aware that their powers depend on various external factors. The date, the day of the week, the position of the zodiac signs, the hour of the day, and the phase of the Moon all affect their power. The color and material of the bag can also directly affect its energies. For example, a charm bag made of animal fur is very common among shamans to make contact with Nature through animals, but the most popular versions today are made of colorful fabric or felt.

Charm bags can contain a number of different objects and a variety of elements that vibrate at the same energetic frequency. For example, a common charm bag for love is a sachet of pink fabric or felt filled with a piece of heart-shaped rose quartz, birch roots, some sandalwood, and scents of musk. After sealing the bag, it is consecrated, or "charged," on a Friday night—the day dedicated to Venus, the goddess of love. Some people may add locks of hair or fingernail clippings to make the bag more personal.

Charm bags are now commonly sold on the Internet, but these have almost certainly not been crafted with appropriate care and according to traditional practice. They often contain substitute ingredients and various items that are chosen with a view toward saving money. These bags tend to be very expensive and are usually ineffective. They, therefore, are not recommended as a very good form of magic.

Charm bags available on the Internet do not, in fact, represent the actual art of charm bags. Although they are cleverly marketed and slickly presented, they are manufactured without due respect for tradition by those without proper spiritual guidance or magical experience. These "commercial" bags normally replace gems, natural crystals, and semi-precious stones with colored glass, and herbs and essential oils—which should be correctly chosen for their characteristics and energetic correspondences—with cheap cologne or perfume. They also sometimes contain regular rocks or the roots of unknown plants. By the standards of traditional magic, this is downright fraudulent.

In part III, you will find instructions for crafting a wide variety of legitimate charm bags that have been tested and proven effective when made with the proper ingredients according to traditional practice. I have also provided lists of all the necessary elements and their properties so you can get creative and come up with your own mixes and combinations for personalized charm bags—for yourself, for a valued friend, or for your loved ones in general.

You don't have to be a special kind of person to create effective charm bags, but your choice of ingredients and your timing—choosing the correct date for enchantment and consecration—is crucial for ensuring that your charm bags have the magical power to effect your purpose.

The Power of Charm Bags

The power of a charm bag depends upon the careful choice of all its various elements—the bag itself, the time it is made, the astrological sign it is made under, the day of the week it is made on, and the herbs, flowers, seeds, colors, essential oils, gems, semi-precious stones, and other items it contains. It also depends on all the circumstances surrounding its construction—mood and feeling, the phase of the Moon, and the focus of the mage performing the ritual.

Charm bags derive their power from the spells that are stored in them. All their energies are channeled through their different components. But in order for its power to be effective, a charm bag must be carried or placed in a specific location—an office, home, bedroom, or garden—where its owner will be in frequent, if not constant, contact with it. If you prepare a charm bag for someone else, that person must carry it or keep it near, because the spell is actually stored in the bag and requires contact to "channel" the energies of the owner. And this works both ways: the owner channels the energies of the bag, and the bag absorbs energy from its owner.

You can make a charm bag for someone who requests it—for instance, a friend who needs a protective amulet for work. Or you may recognize the need for a charm bag in someone else and be inspired to make one—for instance, a little bag to protect your pregnant sister against the Evil Eye that can prevent the envious from having any negative effect on the unborn child. You can also create charm bags as presents—for instance, a bag to bless a newly married couple or a small bag for financial success for someone starting a new job.

Charm Bags and Conventional Spells

A spell consists of a ritual or ceremony that is performed to cause an effect—either a general one, like attracting joy and happiness, or a very specific one, like healing a wound or improving a personal relationship. Despite popular misconceptions, there is no supernatural force involved. You work directly with the forces of Nature to create an entirely *natural* effect that arises from the combination of various elements, aspects, and moments linked fully with certain forces of Nature.

Whether through the rituals used to consecrate them, the charms they contain, or the blessings bestowed on them, all charm bags seek a specific result—sometimes positive; unfortunately, sometimes negative. There are hundreds of forms of spells and rituals, and hundreds of ways to carry them out. Usually, when performing a spell, you grant a "sacrifice" or compensation in order to thank the gods or spirits for their help gaining the desired results—

either to those on the spiritual plane or to various Nature spirits with whom you are working.

When crafting charm bags, however, it is not customary to make any kind of "ritual sacrifice," as you are working with the specific energies of Nature through its different elements. You are simply taking energies that have the same vibration and combining them to achieve a specific result. On the other hand, before consecrating a charm bag, you should be sure to prepare yourself through a brief invocation that seeks the blessings of various deities and higher spirits to ensure that your magical work will achieve the expected results and that nothing will stand in the way of its success.

The charm bag itself is crafted by conducting a short and simple spell, channeling the energies necessary for its success, and storing those energies in a vibrational and integrated form in a small pouch made of cloth, leather, or other material to keep the spell active over a longer period of time. While a conventional spell, once carried out, can be reinforced from time to time by repeating the spell, a charm bag must maintain its power in order to be effective. This is achieved by performing a short version of a spell and storing it permanently within various organic elements that have the same mystical energy vibration as the spell itself and that thus promise to attain the same specific effect.

If you feel an unexpected shift in the energies of a charm bag, you don't need to do the spell all over again. You can simply recharge the bag by placing it on your altar and performing another proper consecration. You can also add a few drops of aromatic oil to it to charge it with more energy. This "recharging" process can even be performed routinely as a kind of "preventive maintenance"—perhaps every week or every month—to keep the spell stored in the bag active and potent.

Likewise, if, for some reason, you want to reinforce the power of your charm bag, you don't need to perform the full spell again.

You can just recharge it with a fairly short ritual and even add an item to it—either to adjust its effects slightly or to reenforce its results. You can do this by carefully opening the bag and adding whatever components you need to increase the bag's power.

If you lose a charm bag, it can be difficult to nullify its effects, but these will lose their balance over time and their power will eventually fade. If you need to nullify a charm bag's magic completely, you can burn it inside a circle of coarse salt. Burn it all the way down to ashes, then bury the ashes. Personally, one of the reasons I like to use charm bags is that I find it reassuring to know that my spell or incantation is stored in there and that I can recharge it or cancel it anytime I feel the need to.

Here is an example of a charm bag to attract love that combines different elements with the same vibrational frequency. Pink candles are commonly used in magic to attract romance and friendship. Roses symbolize true love, and rose oil and petals maintain that same frequency. The scent of musk is widely believed to be endowed with powers that influence attraction. Perform this ritual on a Friday night, because Friday is dedicated to Venus, the Roman goddess of love. This is the night that she is most likely to be attentive to your request.

Charm Bag to Attract Romantic Love
Cast a magic circle and, within it, light pink candles. Fill a small pink cloth bag with some dried roots of rosemary or fir, a rose quartz crystal, and dried rose petals. Anoint the bag with scents of musk or essential oil of roses. Bless this bag with the following magical spell:

At this time and in this place here,

We conjure spirits and avatars of the four cardinal points;

In this place and in this moment here,

We invoke all the energies that favor me to help fulfill the purpose chosen.

Grant my wish and realize my target;

Grant your presence to this ceremony and fill with blessings this ritual.

Alternatively, improvise some words invoking the energies of Venus, the goddess of love and beauty, or the equivalent deity in your own personal pantheon. Carry this sachet with you everywhere. It should only be a matter of time before you begin to feel positive energy flow. You can recharge this charm bag occasionally by annointing it with a few drops of essential oil of roses.

Chapter 6

Crafting and Consecrating Charm Bags

In this chapter, we'll talk about the general practice of crafting charm bags and embuing them with magical power. In part III, you will find instructions for making charm bags targeted on specific effects and goals. But I also encourage you to experiment by making your own charm bags filled with different combinations of elements. Chapters 7 through 11 explain the mystical powers and correspondences of many common elements used in charm bags, including plants, gems, oils, and colors. In the appendices, you will find more information on these elements. Use these lists and descriptions to guide you as you create charm bags for your own personal purposes.

Crafting Charm Bags

Making a charm bag is extremely easy. Just choose your fabric (preferably felt or cotton), being careful to choose one in a color corresponding to your magical goal—for instance, red for love or green for money and riches. (See chapter 7 for a list of color correspondences.) Cut two squares of the fabric, each one smaller than the palm of your hand, then place one square on top of the other and sew three of the four sides together, leaving one side open. Flip the bag inside out to hide the seams. Place the appropriate magical elements within the bag. (See chapters 8 through 11 for guidance in choosing these.) Then seal the bag, either by sewing or by tying the last opening with a ribbon the same color as the bag's fabric. Charge and consecrate the bag using the rituals below, and it is ready for use.

You may want to create your charm bag inside a magic circle. I, personally, believe that casting a magic circle is essential before performing any magical operation at home. The energy of the circle ensures the success of your work and guards against energy dissipation at its conclusion. Magic circles are also often used during rituals of divination or the invocation of other entities. The circle allows you some freedom to interact with the spirits invoked, but does not allow them, or any other spirit in the same path, to cause you harm.

If you are a beginner at magic or simply want to refresh your knowledge, chapter 1 gives instructions on how to make and use a magic circle. Chapter 2 discusses how to make and keep your altar. You must be familiar with these topics before beginning to craft your charm bags. Moreover, the usefulness of these skills is not limited to making charm bags. You can cast a magic circle and keep your altar for all kinds of enchantments, rituals, and sabbaths, and for consecrating different talismans.

Consecrating Charm Bags

In this section, we'll look at two forms of consecration you can use for charging your charm bags—a full consecration ritual for activating charm bags in the comfort and tranquility of your home where you have all the necessary tools available and all the time you need, and a shorter consecration ritual that achieves the same effect, but in a much simpler and more practical way—a "pocket rite" for situations that warrant a quick magical result when you don't have the time to carry out a more elaborate ritual.

The difference in the results of these two methods are evident, however, in both the long and the short term. The full ritual is a full-blown consecration that charges the bag with perfectly channeled elemental energies that achieve an appropriate result. Using this ritual, however, requires proper preparation and a quiet atmosphere in which to work. The shorter ritual is intended for quick action—for instance, to create a charm bag for someone for their birthday, which is to be celebrated that night. The shorter ritual obviously takes less time and preparation, but if you want a good result, it is best to recharge the charm bag within two to three weeks of its creation by performing the ritual again. This helps to channel the energy with which you are working in a more proper and longer-lasting way.

Whether you are using the full ritual or its shorter version, the essential factors to consider when consecrating a charm bag are time, the phase of the Moon, place, and atmosphere and feelings. Although these all work together to ensure the power of your charm bag, let's look at each factor separately so you understand its importance.

Time

Choose the time of day, the day of the week, and even the month of the year that you consider most appropriate for your ceremony. For example, a charm bag intended for clairvoyance or protection can be more effective if consecrated on a Monday (the day of the Moon), while a charm bag for love may be more effective or produce a result that exceeds expectations if consecrated on a Friday (the day of Venus). Appendix C gives you a complete summary of the energetic correspondences for working on every day of the week to achieve your desired results.

Phases of the Moon

The lunar phases and astrological positions are important factors in all magic. And, although these do not directly influence the magic of charm bags, their effects can be seen in your results. For example, while a charm bag consecrated during a New Moon or at the dark of the Moon will achieve its effects, a similar charm bag charged under a Full Moon may be significantly more effective and achieve a more noticeable result. This is because lunar energy influences us most positively when the Moon is at her greatest point and so contributes even more to our rituals.

Although moonlight is considered by many as a pale reflection of sunlight, the Moon has a rather complex and interesting influence over all the inhabitants of the Earth. The Moon rules over life and death. Its inevitable influence is felt in its energetic currents, in wave motion, and in patterns of sleep and rest. Its power is seen in the fertility and growth of all living beings on the planet through its influence on the cycles of menstruation, pregnancy, and childbirth. The Moon thus has mastery over life, growth, and death.

The lunar divinity is divided in popular folklore into three different facets: the virgin maiden (Crescent Moon), the pregnant mother (Full Moon), and the wise crone (waning Moon). The magical personae of Maiden, Mother, and Crone have a strong influence on all forms of magic, whether or not they are linked to sorcery, so it is important to know the role each plays in the performance of effective magic. In chapter 18, you will find lists of lunar correspondences and recommendations for using the lunar phases to support your magic. Be sure to refer to these lists as you begin to craft your charm bags.

- *Crescent Moon*: Symbolizes the pure and virginal young maiden. It is the Moon that emerges from the darkness, representing innocence, purity, curiosity, and restlessness to learn. It is thus the proper lunar phase for starting something new—

for "seeding" a new magical work and seeing how its results emerge from the depths. Because it supports the success of any of your personal aspects, it provides an excellent opportunity for creating your first charm bags and for testing new magic formulas. The Crescent Moon is the ideal time for all those spells and rituals that initiate something new—starting a new romance or bringing good luck to a new endeavor. It is the perfect time to awaken your different hidden qualities and rise from the shadows. It is also a good time for making and blessing all those charm bags that help you achieve something totally new or for those results that require slow but steady growth—a new love, a new job, new friends, and all projects that you hope to expand in the future.

• *Full Moon*: Symbolizes the pregnant mother. It is the Moon pregnant with divine light that is marked with character shining overhead. It represents maturity, commitment, character, and constant learning. This is the time to enjoy your achievements and successes and to celebrate goals accomplished. It is the time to see all your aspirations and dreams come true. The Full Moon is perhaps the lunar phase most used in magic to carry out spells and rituals that seek to transform or transmute. It is the most appropriate moment for performing all spells and rituals that are linked to balance, equilibrium, harmony, and stability. This is the most powerful phase of the Moon and has the potential to transmute all aspects of your life. It is the phase that stimulates and strengthens all spells and rituals, and is the perfect time to make charm bags designed by you from scratch, once you have gained enough experience to do so.

• *Waning Moon*: Symbolizes the wise crone constantly resting. It is the Moon that has aged and is about to disappear from the firmament. It represents old age, experience, disease, tranquility, inner peace, rest, and death. It invites you to conclude, quickly close, and consolidate all your magical works and finish consecrating your talismans. It is the time for creating charm bags that close or reduce something, that cancel a spell or curse, and that reduce the power of a warlock or an evil witch who seeks to harm you through esoteric means. During the waning Moon, light fades. It is the time to perform magic spells that nullify curses, hexes, and negative feelings, to ward off impure thoughts and distractions, and to eliminate all sorts of vices. Next to the Full Moon, it is perhaps the best time for séances that seek to banish spirits and send them back to their source.

- *New Moon*: Symbolizes emptiness and nothingness. It is the Moon that rests on the past before being reborn. These are the darkest times for witchcraft. Divination becomes slower and more confusing. Witches may feel they have lost part of their connection with Nature. The spirits may cause an uproar because it is a time of confusion for them and the souls of the dead often lose touch with their dear ones. It is the right time to meditate and analyze your projects in detail, and the best time to start new projects. This is the time to reflect on new forces that are coming into your life—a time of awareness, reflection, and awakening. During the New Moon, rest from your magic temporarily and dedicate yourself to study, reflection, and research. Your magic may retain its power, but that power will be more noticeable when the Moon manifests itself again. The New Moon is thus an experimental phase, when you can sketch and plan your next steps in magic in careful detail—when you can search for all the elements, tools, and magical implements you will need to produce your charm bags and study the best time for crafting and consecrating them.

Place

It is important to choose the most appropriate place to consecrate your charm bags. This place is usually your personal altar but could be any large space with neutral colors and a fresh and quiet ambience. Unfortunately, it is often very difficult, for a variety of reasons, to find spaces like this, so many resort to their altars. But remember that you can perform any kind of spell or ritual in any enclosed space without diminishing its effectiveness, provided that you prepare the site with some incense and maintain order and tranquility in the area where you will work. In fact, the kitchen seems to be a good place to perform all kinds of rituals and has been the favorite place for many witches in the world. One popular saying claims: "The kitchen is the corner of the home where women prepare food during the day and all manner of magical brews at night."

Atmosphere and Mood

All rituals and magical ceremonies should be performed in an atmosphere of tranquility and inner calm. In fact, in magic, inner peace is your greatest ally. Do not try to cast spells if you feel frustrated or depressed, unless it is a ritual or amulet to help combat precisely this situation. Nor should you try to perform any kind of ritual or ceremony if you feel stressed, because this will interfere with your concentration and focus. The most likely outcome in that situation is that you won't channel the right energy and will end up spoiling the whole ritual.

Feelings are important in magic. They are a source of holistic energy and a powerful stimulant for each individual practitioner. When performing a ritual or consecration, use your emotions to help you focus your energies. Think of the ritual you are performing with positivity and faith, and do not let any negative emotion intervene in the proceedings. Before you begin, dispel your worries and let your positive emotions influence the ritual and amulets by transmitting to them your joy and positive attitude.

Consecration Rituals

There are two ways to consecrate a charm bag: with a full ritual or a short one. If you have the time and space, it is best to use the full ritual, as it will ensure that your charm bags are properly blessed and consecrated. First, choose the most appropriate date to perform the ritual, remembering that the energy of this date and hour is what will empower and activate the magic of your charm bag.

Full Consecration Ritual

Before beginning, fill a bowl with clean water and add a few drops of an appropriate essential oil. (See chapter 10 for a summary of essential oils and their corresponding energies.) You will use this during the ritual, mixing the water with your fingers and anointing your hands with it to embue yourself with its energy.

Draw a magic circle on the floor using chalk, coarse salt, a mixture of dry herbs, or a consecrated rope. (See chapter 1 for information on all these different methods.) Remember to trace the circle in a clockwise direction. Then place everything you need for your ritual inside the circle. You can also consecrate your bag within a circle on your altar or on a makeshift altar inside the circle. Either one is a valid method and both are quite common.

Prepare your altar with elements, colors, and symbols appropriate for the charm bag you want to consecrate. Have on hand three sticks or cones of the aromatic incense recommended for the bag's purpose. If you don't have a particular incense, you can use another one with qualities and spiritual correspondences similar to it. Light the first stick or cone before you draw the magic circle to purify the environment of any energy or entity that may hinder your ritual in any way. You will light the second one during the ceremony to activate the energies and channel them through the charm bag. You will burn the third when the ritual is complete to give thanks to the spirits and deities who were present.

To channel the four elements, use a candle for each color of Nature—white in the east to channel the Air element, red in the south to channel the Fire element, blue in the west to channel the Water element, and green or brown in the north to channel the Earth element. Place a fifth candle in the center—either white or purple—to channel the ether and spiritual energy. This center candle can also be gold or silver if you want to channel the energy of the Sun or the Moon. (See appendix E for a full description of candle magic and its possibilities for consecrating charm bags.)

Place a saucer in your ritual space with a little rock salt and dirt in it to strengthen the power of the Nature spirits at the site, and a glass or cup of water to which you can add a drop or two of essential oil to turn it into ritual water.

Perform a brief meditation before you begin if you need to relax. Then light the second piece of incense to begin the ritual. Light the candles one by one and begin to consecrate all the elements and tools that will make up your charm bag, each in its turn—herbs, gems, flowers, metals, etc. Pick them up one by one and anoint them with a few drops of the essential oil you chose for the ritual.

Place all the anointed items in the pouch you made, one by one, charging each with positive thoughts and focusing on your expected results. Hold each one with both hands and recite the following incantation:

Oh, great ancient Gods and coming Spirits,
Protective souls and familiar sorcerers,
In this moment, we call upon Thee.
In this place, give Thy essential services;
In this ritual, I implore Thee,

In the name of the solemn sooth.
Make presence in my own charm circle,
Make presence here in my own locale,
At this witching hour, I beg Thee,
Pass with your good thoughts
Through my own ritual circle,
And with Thy most wondrous powers,
Grant spiritual communion.
Please lend Thy support now and forever,
Give Thy blessing to this artifact of Nature
Turn this object that I present Thee today
Into a powerful tool of Great White Magic
And awaken its charmed soul to the practice.
Oh, great coming Spirits of the East,
Wind Gods and avatars of knowledge,
Ye who ruleth over all things creative,
Give Thy blessing to this powerful talisman
Which I craft today to reach contentment.
Oh, great coming Spirits of the South,
Fire Gods and avatars of love and war,
Ye who ruleth over all human thought,
Give Thy blessing to this powerful charm
Which I craft today to reach delight.
Oh, great coming Spirits of the West,
Gods of oceans, High Magic, and rivers,
Rulers of all living things in this world,
Give Thy blessing to this powerful talisman
Which I craft today to reach happiness.
Oh, great coming Spirits of the North,
Gods of the Earth and avatars of Earth,
Ye who ruleth alike over man and beast,
Give Thy blessing to this powerful talisman
Which I craft today to reach contentment.

Once the incantation is finished, seal the charm bag completely, either by tying or sewing the ends. As a symbolic presentation to the elements, pass the bag through the incense smoke to receive the blessing of Air. Pass it with great care around the flame of the red candle to receive the blessing of Fire. Anoint it with a few drops of water from the cup to receive the blessing of Water. And pass it over the saucer with salt and soil in it to receive the blessing of Earth. Always pass the bag around the candle flame in a clockwise direction.

After the consecration ceremony is finished, hold the charm bag against your chest for a few moments, then place it on a white saucer or a piece of white cloth to allow the positive energies to become entrenched without any interference. Offer a brief thanks to free choice, then thank all the spirits, deities, and avatars who were present, as well as those entities who may, unknown to you, have given their blessing or who, for some reason, may not have been present during the ritual.

To close the ceremony, burn the last piece of incense. Leave the consecrated charm bag in the location you have chosen, and collect and clean all the elements you used, as well as your altar—the wax from the candles, for instance. If you wish, you can freshen your charm bag with a few drops of essential oil of sandalwood or myrrh every Friday night to keep it charged.

Short Consecration Ritual

If, for any reason, you do not have enough time to perform this full consecration ritual, you can use this alternative ritual in many different situations. With this shorter ritual, you can consecrate and activate your charm bags in a simple and practical way. This ritual is also ideal for consecrating your first charm bags, because you can use it to gain experience before attempting the more extensive and complex ritual given above. This is a short adaptation of the full ritual that is simple and easy to memorize. You can use it in different places or situations.

Begin by drawing a magic circle on the floor. If you do not have enough space, create a small ritual circle using a consecrated rope or some chalk and salt. This will help channel the energies you need into one place for the ritual you are performing.

Light a stick of incense—either sandalwood or a fragrance that corresponds to the energy you want to channel. Light a candle of the corresponding ritual color. If you don't have the right color candle, a white candle is always useful for channeling most energies basically anywhere.

Bless each of the elements to be used in your bag—herbs, oils, stones, etc.—with a few drops of the appropriate essential oil and add them one by one to the bag you have prepared. Then pass the charm bag through the incense smoke several times in a clockwise direction while you say the following incantation aloud three times:

> At this time and in this place here,
> We conjure spirits and avatars of the four cardinal points.
> In this place and in this moment here,
> We invoke all the energies that favor me to help fulfill the
> purpose chosen.
> Grant my wish and realize my target;
> Grant your presence to this ceremony and fill with blessings
> this ritual.

Then completely close the bag.

After finishing the consecration, set the charm bag aside and allow the candle and incense to burn down completely. Do not extinguish them. Offer thanks in your own words to the spirits and deities you invoked to perform the ritual. Don't forget to recharge the charm bag after a few weeks, anointing the outside of the bag with a few drops of the appropriate essential oil.

Chapter 7

Using Colors in Charm Bags

Color is the visual perception we have of the different lengths of light waves that constantly surround us. Light waves are broken into a range of lengths through reflection and refraction in the atmosphere, and these different length rays are what we perceive as color with the human eye. White contains the complete range of color, while the absence of color is perceived as black. Between black and white lies a spectrum of what we call "primary" colors— the colors of the rainbow—that can themselves be broken down into a range of shades and gradations, depending on the reflection and refraction of the light rays creating them.

Colors are the main components of the visual arts. They are the "language" of painting and graphic design, of photography and printing, and even of television and cinema. Colors influence us in many ways in every moment. They affect us emotionally as well as spiritually. Research has shown that the diversity and use of colors in different situations can significantly affect peoples' moods. In fact, some theorize that there are no naturally blue fruits, because the color blue encourages a feeling of satiety. As Nature evolved, these researchers say, it stopped creating blue fruits because of their lack of a role in the food chain. Recently, nutritionists have recommended using blue dishes, because when we eat from blue dishes, we feel satisfied more quickly and therefore eat less. Likewise, restaurants tend to use dishes of different shades of orange and yellow, because these colors tend to increase the appetite so people will eat more. In hospitals, neutral colors are used to provide a sense of calm for patients and their family members. Schools decorate in lighter shades of green and blue to promote calm and a feeling of comfort among students, while spiritual centers commonly use white and gold to create a sense of purity and majesty.

The Greek philosopher Aristotle believed that "basic colors" were somehow linked to the elements of Earth, Fire, Water, and Air. Centuries later, European alchemists still studied color as a representation of the elements of Nature. The Austrian alchemist Paracelsus even went so far as to associate colors with the chemical elements, the elements of Nature, and the elemental spirits. Color, he argued, put us in touch with the elements and their corresponding elementals. Red linked us metaphysically to Fire and salamanders; yellow linked us to the wind and sylphs; blue linked us to Water and mermaids; and green allowed us to channel Earth and gnomes.

The Maya in Central America associated the cardinal points—north, south, east, and west—with red, yellow, black, and white, and saw these as the representative colors of the guardian gods of each direction. In fact, throughout history, scholars—for instance, Goethe in his treatise *Color Theory* and Eva Heller in *The True Story of All Colors*—have concluded that color, even beyond its physical qualities—is strongly associated with various aspects of human emotion, claiming that the different colors we perceive around us link us to symbols, specific emotions, and socially accepted meanings that enable us to channel or produce different energies and effects.

Today, psychologists study colors to discover how they are linked to our moods, our health, and our attitudes. And in magic and sorcery, these linkages become especially significant because they, in turn, link us to different planes of existence and different levels of understanding. We live in a universe surrounded by different colors. We see colors every second of our daily lives—colors that, in magic and ritual, come to represent symbolic and energetic functions. In candle magic, for instance, practitioners must understand the influence of different colors in order to bring those influences to bear on other aspects of their lives (see appendix E).

When crafting and consecrating charm bags, it is very important to understand the role of colors and to work with their different symbolic meanings. When you choose the appropriate color for a charm bag, or for the elements in it, you channel the correct energy for achieving its purpose and ensure the success of the bag you are crafting. Make sure that the bag itself is made of a material whose color corresponds to its function and the effect you hope to create. For example, a charm bag for love should be red or pink, depending on the type of love you want to attract, while a charm bag to cleanse and purify your aura should be white, the color that represents purity. Indeed, I cannot overstress how important it is to use the right colors when crafting your charm bags. Color can determine the success of the effect you want to accomplish, and the use of an inappropriate color can easily spoil what would otherwise be a good charm bag.

Magical Properties of Colors

Here is a brief summary of the magical properties of the colors most commonly used in charm bags.

- **Black**: dispels sadness, depression, fear, melancholy, and fatigue. Also protects against evil spells, witchcraft, and all forms of evil.

- **Blue**: encourages sympathy, friendship, peace, freedom, confidence, and independence.

- **Brown**: encourages maturity, diplomacy, character, regeneration, and physical strength, and channels the healing energies of the Earth.

- **Gold**: attracts material wealth, abundance, pride, satisfaction, and happiness, and channels the energies of the solar god.

- **Green**: attracts health, success, stability, and hope. Also channels the energies of Gaia, Mother Nature, and the spirits of the forest.

- **Indigo**: strengthens or stimulates psychic powers, telepathy, intuition, clairvoyance, and extrasensory perception.

- **Mulberry**: brings positive change to certain aspects of your own personality. Also supports hobbies and dispels bad vices.

- **Orange**: attracts joy, positive vibrations, creativity, intelligence, sociability, and charisma.

- **Pink**: attracts pure love, romance, eroticism, charm, friendship, and emotional sensitivity.

- **Purple**: increases focus on transmuting energies in negative or complex situations that seem difficult to solve.

- **Red**: attracts love, passion, vitality, vigor, desire, and sexuality.

- **Silver**: attracts promotion, respect, protection, and stability. Also strengthens clairvoyance and the psyche, and channels the energies of the Moon goddess.

- **Violet**: supports spells related to justice, legal documents, and transactions and proceedings of all kinds. Also channels the energies of the spiritual world more effectively.

- **White**: attracts calm, peace, wisdom, purification, and health, and encourages mental and spiritual development.

- **Yellow**: attracts joy, happiness, fun, kindness, curiosity, and creativity.

Chapter 8

Using Plants and Herbs in Charm Bags

Throughout history, witches have believed that, somehow, Nature can cure all—that Nature is our best doctor and that we must honor her. Witches and great magicians found their powers in Nature, believing that the enormous forces of the natural elements can heal us physically, mentally, emotionally, and spiritually.

And in fact, Mother Gaia is like a good mother who is always there for us. She asks for only one thing in return—respect. Yet, we have not always accorded her that respect. We seem to have the shameful idea that the Earth is ours and that it depends on us, rather than the other way around. But this is not true. We must take care of the Earth because Mother Gaia will still be here, strong and glorious, long after we are dead and gone. On the other hand, if we do not nurture her and care for her, she will perish, and we will undoubtedly perish with her.

Mother Gaia was here long before we were and has survived and evolved through the onslaughts of previous civilizations as well as the predations of our own. Yet she persists. We still do not know the limits of her powers. Indeed, a wise man once said that the healing power of Nature is as vast as the stupid human idea that man is the ruler of all things. Whatever the larger truth, Nature is here, ready to serve us, with millions of plants and herbs and flowers that provide us with myriad remedies for the evils in the world.

Magical Properties of Plants and Herbs

The world of Nature gives us many basic remedies like garlic, onion, lemon, green tea, and aloe vera that are used in natural medicine and in the kitchen. As a practitioner of magic, you must study the healing properties of these plants and all others so that you can heal yourself and help and advise others when necessary. The following is a formulary of natural plants and herbs with their magical correspondences and energetic effects:

- *Acacia (Acacia sensu lato)*: protects against all evil; burn it to frighten away demons and evil spirits, and to attract love, good fortune, and money. Its flowers are commonly used to decorate altars in honor of the African deity Oshun.

- *Aconite (Aconitum napellus)*: wards off evil spirits and annoying entities. *Note*: Roots of different species can be toxic and/or poisonous.

- *Alder (Alnus serrulata)*: strengthens invocations and empowers enchanted items.

- *Alfalfa (Medicago sativa)*: improves focus and keeps you targeted on a purpose; linked to the magic of desires; use to balance the household economy.

- *Almond (Prunus dulcis)*: strengthens rituals associated with prosperity; attracts wisdom, helps make decisions, and cancels shame and fear. Its dried flowers attract wisdom, strengthen intuition, and develop the psyche; its fruits (almonds) attract prosperity and symbolize abundance.

- **Aloe vera (Aloe)**: grants healing powers to sorcerers and guards against the Evil Eye and envy; prohibits spirits from entering your home without being summoned; has a wide range of therapeutic uses.

- **Angelica (Angelica archangelica)**: masters the mind and puts aside personal fears; repels all sorts of curses, spells, and incantations. The dry root of angelica stimulates healing.

- **Anise (Pimpinella anisum)**: strengthens all magical rituals; attracts luck in gambling and stimulates the powers of a magician; also known for its cleansing and healing powers.

- **Apple (Pyrus malus)**: empowers all forms of love and protection magic. Apple blossoms provide protection and strengthen concentration; use dried to complement protection bags.

- **Arnica (mountain arnica)**: has magical qualities associated with invocation and the art of hypnosis. Its flowers can be combined with other plants to create a powerful magic circle of invocation. *Note*: May be poisonous.

- **Ash tree (Fraxinus ornus)**: protects from all evil. In Norse mythology, the ash tree helped create the mead that sustained the Vikings on their journey to Valhalla. In Europe, drawing circles on the ground with branches of ash was believed to ward off snakes.

- **Azahar (orange blossom)**: white flowers of the orange tree; clears negative thoughts, protects caring lovers, and detects lies; also excellent in perfumery.

- **Basil (Ocimum basilicum)**: has powers related to love, fidelity, peace, happiness, protection, and divination.

- **Belladonna (Atropa belladona)**: calms headaches and menstrual symptoms; protects against evil; known as the witches' herb. *Note*: Belladonna is poisonous.

- **Benzoin (Lindera benzoin)**: blesses ritual spaces and private homes; has protective qualities.

- **Bergamot (Citrus bergamia)**: attracts money and empowers prosperity spells that invoke good fortune; brings luck in economics and employment.

- **Birch (Betula pendula)**: has powers related to love, protection, and divination; wards off evil influences, counters all sorts of spells, and protects pregnant women.

- **Bismalva (hollyhock mallow; Malva alcea;)**: dried flowers strengthen health; has a wide range of medical uses.

- **Bryonia (Bryonia alba)**: guards against any danger; locates lost and hidden treasures.

- **Burdock (Arctium lappa)**: attracts prosperity and satisfaction. Its flowers symbolize prosperity and abundance. In Turkey, used as an amulet to avoid the Evil Eye; widely used in Traditional Chinese Medicine to purge blood.

- **Calendula (Calendula officinalis)**: conjures love, friendship, and affection; encourages respect and promotions.

- **Camellia (Camellia sinesensis)**: supports all spells and rituals associated with angelic magic; eradicates poltergeists.

- **Camphor (Cinnamomum camphora)**: wards off evil and negative vibrations; supplements charm bags with protection magic; use to draw a magic circle for any magical operation.

- **Carnation (Dianthus caryophyllus)**: highly effective in love magic. Often used to complement spells and charm bags linked to love, fidelity, fertility, and romance.

- **Catnip (Nepeta cataria)**: attracts good luck, beauty, and passion; used in sachets to strengthen feelings of love.

- **Cedar (Cedrus)**: attracts money; purifies; eliminates nightmares and protects against harm.

- **Chamomile (German chamomile)**: attracts calm, patience, and prosperity; its flowers bring good luck and naturally appease.

- **Cherry tree (Prunus avium)**: known for its powers of protection; use in spells to care for someone far away; protects personal property and blesses wills.

- **Chicory (blue dandelion; common chicory)**: bypasses certain kinds of vibrations and negative manifestations; strengthens personal protection.

- **Cinnamon (Cinnamonum verum)**: naturally related to love and all sorts of enchantments and illusions; protects and wards off thieves; use to obtain employment and to strip away the bad energy in irrigation systems and personal bathrooms.

- **Clove (Syzygium aromaticum)**: powerful aphrodisiac; useful for finding family and for protection against envy.

- **Clover (Trifolium)**: attracts health, good fortune, love, and prosperity. A clover in your wallet ensures you'll never lack money; a clover on your altar ensures that all your spells will succeed.

- *Coffee (Coffea arabica)*: protects against gnomes and crawling spirits; clears rooms of bad energies and takes care of household pets.

- *Copal (Protium copal)*: aromatic vegetable resin used in traditional indigenous medicine; nullifies negativity and depressive thoughts.

- *Coriander (cilantro; Coriandrum sativum)*: related to sexual magic, the magic of protection, and purification; often combined with rue and rosemary to protect the home and its inhabitants.

- *Cumin (Cuminum cyminum)*: promotes love and friendship; add to charm bags to protect the family and home.

- *Cyclamen (Cyclamen persicum)*: fights evil and destroys negative spells.

- *Cypress (Cypressus sempervirens)*: symbolizes immortality and wisdom; its oil is widely used to consecrate and bless talismans and magical objects; use in charm bags to protect and care for a loved one.

- *Daffodil (Narcissus poeticus)*: flowers bring peace of mind and harmony; essential in charm bags to attract tranquility and to calm anger or bad temper.

- *Dandelion (Taraxacum officinale)*: flowers support divination and rituals to manifest desires; burn it to dispel evil.

- *Dill (Anethum graveolens)*: destroys powerful curses and Voodoo dolls.

- *Dragon's blood (Dracanea draco)*: wards off enemies and attracts friends; also has the power to break all kinds of curses and spells, even at a distance.

- **Elder (elderberry; Sambucus)**: widely known for its rugged appearance and diverse medicinal uses; also known in witchcraft and white magic for its protective qualities. Burn small parts of it to ward off evil spirits; berries are used in charm bags to exorcize evil.

- **Eucalyptus (Eucaliptus globulus)**: calms tension and the nerves; believed to have the power to influence the minds and memories of others; use to attract new and interesting friendships.

- **Fir (Abies magnifica)**: brings prosperity and protection; also used to care for children.

- **Gardenia (Gardenia jasminoides)**: dried petals added to magical sachets to attract love and increase the attraction of the opposite sex.

- **Garlic (Allium sativum)**: brings good luck and protects against the Evil Eye, envy, and spells; wards off evil and protects the home from thieves and unpleasant visits; commonly used in exorcisms and healings.

- **Geranium (Geranium maderense)**: supports all spells related to love, fertility, virility, and sexuality; also for protection and divination.

- **Ginger (Zingiber officinale)**: has great health properties; attracts passion and improves health. Use ginger oil to strengthen charm bags designed to rekindle the flame of a romantic relationship. *Note*: Do not confuse with wild ginger from North America, which is highly carcinogenic.

- **Ginseng (Panax quinquefolius)**: known for its medicinal and stimulant properties; used in witchcraft for protection and invocation; dried in the sun and crushed, it yields a magic powder for protection; also often burned as incense to spirits. Add in small amounts to any charm bag to strengthen its magic.

- *Hazel (Corylus avellana)*: strengthens spells related to intuition, calm, divination, and clairvoyance.

- *Heather (ling; Calluna vulgaris)*: blesses and supports all kinds of businesses and shops; its powers are linked to the magic of the forest spirits, so it is effective when invoking them.

- *Heliotrope (Heliotropium arborescens)*: essential for charm bags to attract clairvoyance and strengthen divination; useful as an oil to clean and purify glass spheres and pendulums.

- *Hemp-leaved hollyhock (Althaea rosea)*: flowers strengthen clairvoyance and protect homes. A brown or yellow bag filled with it and hung on the door keeps away envy and people with bad intentions.

- *Henbane (nightshade; Hyoscyamus niger)*: invokes higher spirits and strengthens mental powers; a variation (black henbane) is associated with the power of witches and can balance or cancel all kinds of spells.

- *Hibiscus (flower cayenne; Hibiscus)*: use to decorate altars and burn as incense to improve health; use in charm bags for protection.

- *Holly (Ilex aquifolium)*: protects against the Evil Eye and wards off bad luck; also attracts good fortune and blesses talismans.

- *Hollyhocks (Alcea rosea)*: improves health and dispels evil; very suitable for charm bags that channel protection and health.

- **Holm oak (Quercus ilex)**: considered a sacred tree in many religions; associated with longevity and high spirituality. A sprig of holm oak, or a charm bag containing one, will bring money and good luck.

- **Honeysuckle (Lonicera)**: widely used in Traditional Chinese Medicine and modern homeopathy; attracts prosperity and good fortune; in green charm bags, accelerates the action of any spell and awakens the magic dormant within you.

- **Hyacinth (Hyacinthus orientalis)**: attracts love and friendship.

- **Hyssop (Hysoppus officinalis)**: widely used in medicine and perfumery; parts of hyssop added to a charm bag promote healthy finances, income, wealth, and financial success.

- **Jasmine (Jasminium officinalis)**: has powers of purification, invocation, and protection; attracts love and wards off nightmares.

- **Juniper (Juniperus communis)**: guards against accidents and betrayals.

- **Laurel (Laurus nobilis)**: cleanses the aura, eases pain, and attracts good omens; inspires poets and artists and brings good fortune to their hosts; protects against evil at any time.

- **Lavender (Lavandula augustifolia)**: known for its cleansing powers; banishes evil and calms thoughts; burn its flowers to facilitate astral projection and all kinds of meditation.

- **Lemon (Citrus limonum)**: effective for casting spells of protection and to ward off evil; add dried lemon peel and seeds to charm bags to attract positive vibrations.

- **Lemon balm (melissa; Melissa officinalis)**: has strong citrus aroma and soothing properties that act as a natural painkiller when brewed as a tea. Its essential oil is widely used in perfumery. Add lemon balm to charm bags to attract money, wealth, good fortune, and success in any financial field.

- **Lily (Lilium candidum)**: wards off evil, negativity, envy, and jealousy; use in charm bags to protect against bad intentions and to encourage calm and serenity; wards off depression and protects courtships and marriages.

- **Lotus (Nelumbo nucifera)**: widely used for protection and purification; use as an aromatic oil to bless magical tools and altars. Its incense brings peace and protection; in a charm bag, it attracts blessings and good luck.

- **Magnolia (Magnolia virginiana)**: dried flowers stimulate tranquility, inner peace, calm, and psychic development; in a charm bag, strengthens clairvoyance and mental relaxation during meditation.

- **Mandrake (Mandragora officinarum)**: controls negative energies, wards off envy, and purifies thoughts; use to attract, dominate, and exorcize all kinds of spirits and demons; increases magical powers and allows the summoning of the dead; one of the best-known plants of witches.

- **Marjoram (Origanum majorana)**: protects against emotional wounds, tension, and stress; protects against evil.

- **Mimosa (sleepy plant; Mimosa pudica)**: flower and oils widely used to promote deep meditation and healing; in South America, a charm bag that contains mimosa placed under a pillow attracts prophetic dreams and visions from other planes.

- *Mint (Mentha spicata)*: brings good luck, money, and prosperity; use to cancel spells.

- *Mistletoe (Viscum album)*: encourages health, love, positive energy, and magical protection; grants wishes, protects faithful couples, and brings wealth and good humor.

- *Mugworth (Artemisia vulgaris)*: a protective herb par excellence, its magic is intimately linked to the spirits of the forest. This plant is dedicated to St. John the Baptist.

- *Musk (Mimulus moschatus; Abelmoschus moschatus)*: popularly used for purification rituals and spells. Is the perfect ingredient for the charm bags to channel love, for protection, and to strengthen divination.

- *Mustard (Sinapis alba)*: unquestionable powers of protection; works in all rituals to care for and protect people, homes, vehicles, etc.

- *Myrrh (Commiphora myrra)*: aromatic resin highly valued in ancient times for use in perfumes, incense, ointments, creams, medicines, and more. It is widely used today as an incense or aromatic oil to consecrate all kinds of magical altars, tools, and talismans. Add to a charm bag to protect against evil spells and hexes, or use as an oil to consecrate gems and dried herbs.

- *Nettle (Urtica dioica)*: known since antiquity as the "grass of the blind" for its ability to produce a terrible irritation and intense itching on contact with the skin; use (carefully) in charm bags as an aphrodisiac. *Note*: Not recommended for common use because of its irritant properties.

- *Oak (Quercus robur)*: restores health, brings protection and good luck, protects against disease, and boosts sexual energy.

- **Orange (Citrus aurantium)**: burn flowers and leaves to promote clairvoyance and give an atmosphere of peace and protection; add the peel, flowers, and seeds to charm bags to attract love and happiness, and strengthen the love in a relationship.

- **Oregano (Origanum vulgare)**: known for its culinary uses as well as for dispelling coughs; add to charm bags that purify or that offer peace and spiritual calm to the wearer.

- **Palo santo (Bulnesia sarmientoi)**: burned as a tribute to the gods to ward off evil spirits; used to exorcize all kinds of demons and malicious spirits. Use it to complement a magic circle of protection; use its oil to perfume charm bags to ward off evil.

- **Parsley (Petroselinum crispum)**: excellent choice for charm bags dedicated to protection; burn it by the door to ward off evil.

- **Patchouli (Pogostemon cablin)**: use as an incense, oil, or aromatic herb to attract prosperity and abundance, as well as to cure infertility; use in charm bags to attract inner peace and tranquility.

- **Pathbreaking (siguaraya; Trichilia havanensis)**: widely used in modern currents of spiritism to open the path for those who carry it, and to close the path to enemies. According to folklore, contains the essences of the seven African divinities of creation.

- **Pine (Pinus)**: excellent choice for charm bags that strengthen the capacity to perform magic; stimulates clairvoyance and strengthens all sorts of spells.

- **Poppy (Papaver)**: conjures love and money, and empowers various amulets and talismans.

- **Raspberry (Rubus idaeus)**: add sundried raspberries to charm bags that stimulate sexuality and love and for all kinds of aphrodisiac purposes.

- **Rose (Rosa)**: influences all rituals related to love and indifference; attracts love, engenders love in someone specific, dims memory of a past love, and wards off unwanted lovers; also brings peace and protection.

- **Rosemary (Rosmarinus officinalis)**: improves memory and concentration; protects places, objects, animals, and people. Brings good luck if carried in a purse; use to extend youth spells.

- **Rue (herb of grace; Ruta graveolens)**: plant close to your home to ward off evil and all sorts of curses; brewed as a tea with chamomile, it dispels a headache. Use in spells to bring love and peace to the home.

- **Saffron (Crocus sativa)**: protects against misfortunes and dangers in the streets; protects mothers and children and eases the strain on the environment.

- **Sage (Salvia)**: increases wisdom, prolongs life, and protects against the Evil Eye; attracts good luck; use to visualize the future. An infusion of the flowers sprinkled on the doors and windows of a house can reveal secrets and hidden enemies.

- **Sagebrush (true artemisia; Artemisia tridentata)**: for protection and divination; strengthens clairvoyance and the ability to see what is hidden; protects children. Drunk in a tea or infusion, it develops clairvoyance and clairaudience. Use it to see forest spirits and perceive all kinds of psychic manifestations. Burn as an incense to keep away evil spirits.

- *Sandalwood (chandanam; Santalum album)*: known for its exquisite aroma; has great powers of protection. This plant governs the magic of love; use in incense to purify.

- *Savory (Satureja hortensis)*: resolves gastronomic problems through its aromatic qualities; add to charm bags to promote rapid healing and prolong life.

- *Sesame (Sesamum indicum)*: use as a supplement for spells, rituals, and protective amulets; add seeds to a personalized charm bag for greater power.

- *St. John's wort (Hypericum perforatum)*: relieves depression and sadness; burn it to ward off evil spirits and demons. Known as "the exorcist plant."

- *Strawberry (Fragaria virginiana)*: essential to all talismans, spells, and potions that channel the energy of love, seduction, or sexual attraction; use as an aromatic oil to protect households and people.

- *Sunflower (helianthus; Helianthus annuus)*: dried flowers provide spiritual peace and bring wealth; add to charm bags to conjure good fortune and success of projects.

- *Tangerine (Citrus tangerina)*: attracts friendship and develops personal gifts; wards off goblins.

- *Thyme (Thymus vulgaris)*: attracts good health; wards off nightmares and has powers of protection. Use in talismans to help them retain their energy.

- *Vanilla (Vanilla planifolia)*: renowned for its unique aroma and flavor; aphrodisiac; use for spells linked to love, protection, and improvement of the intellect. Burn as an incense to recover lost energies after performing a ritual; use in charm bags to attract peace and psychic power.

- **Verbena (vervain; Verbena officinalis)**: powerful protection and purification plant that is impervious to evil; wards off warlocks and demons. Use in rituals and talismans for protection and to bless and purify household altars.

- **Vetiver (Vetiveria zizanoides)**: used in modern perfumery because of its exquisite fragrance; use oil to anoint talismans to attract money and channel success. Can be combined with sandalwood and oak in a green charm bag to attract prosperity and good fortune.

- **Violet (Viola odorata)**: used by witches to override weak spells and eliminate headaches; attracts love and friendship.

- **Vitis (Vid; Vitis vinifera)**: all parts of this plant support magic related to love, abundance, and attraction; also stimulates imagination and love.

- **Willow (Saliz babylonica)**: all parts of all varieties are known for their protective powers; burn it as an incense to ward off evil and accompany exorcisms. Weeping willow (willow of Babylon) wards off unknown evils and is impervious to evil. Use goat willow in rites that protect the home and white willow as an analgesic and anti-inflammatory. Use to strengthen charm bags intended to ward off evil thoughts, jealousy, and envy.

- **Wormwood (Artemisia absinthium)**: this plant is often burned at night to honor the Moon gods; used to drive away demons, witches, and evil spirits; also protects against the Evil Eye. In Mexico, it is widely used in meditations to stimulate the fertility of women.

- *Yarrow (Achillea millefolium)*: also known as grass of Achilles and Roman chamomile; linked to the goddess Venus and used for spells and rituals to bring happiness to the heart. Burn it as an incense or add to a ritual bath. Removes negativity in surroundings and brings courage and friendship; helps you make good decisions. A charm bag containing yarrow and roses, prepared on a Friday night, attracts love and happiness.

- *Yew (Taxus baccata)*: known in South America as "the cemetery guardian"; extremely long-lived and linked to death and immortality. Some legends link it to a spell to summon spirits and deities from beyond. Use the fruits in charm bags to prolong life. *Note*: Extremely toxic.

- *Ylang ylang (Cananga odorata)*: widely used in aromatherapy as a calming agent and aphrodisiac. Add to charm bags intended for love and sexual attraction.

Chapter 9

Using Gems and Stones in Charm Bags

The magic of gems is vast and plays a role in most spiritual traditions and folklore. Charm bags used in white magic and witchcraft usually contain some sort of gemstone. Others use gems and crystals during consecration ceremonies. Many sorcerers and mages give crystals or stones to their friends and families for protection, healing, or success.

Gems all channel the Earth element, which is embraced in magic, but, because they all have different energetic vibrations, you must make sure when using them that their energies work toward your purpose. Amber and translucent quartz have similar vibrations, for instance, and they become charged with magical power when you bless them in a short ritual. This starts them vibrating in your own frequency, which turns them into a personal talisman with powers that work in your favor.

As with all magical elements, the astrological energy and the phase of the Moon on the day a gemstone is blessed have a strong influence on the magical properties it acquires. For example, a meteor shower has the power to conjure more magic and influence in your life, while the Full Moon helps consolidate long-term projects. The most powerful time to bless gemstones and crystals is

Samhain (Hallowe'en or All Hallows' Eve), because this popular holiday marks the night when magic, Nature, and the universe start renewing their powers. Old energies are renewed and new ones are as strong as they will ever be. The barrier that separates spiritual planes is thinner during the week of Samhain, giving us easier access to the magic of other worlds. The Blue Moon is another propitious time for blessing gemstones and crystals. It is a lunar event of great magnitude and enormous power that occurs only occasionally, unlike Samhain, which happens every year at the same time.

The important thing is to choose a date that corresponds to the intent you have for the gemstone—for example, an amulet to confront and disarm an enemy is better blessed on Tuesday, the day dedicated to Mars, the god of war. A stone to be used to attract love has greater magical energy and effect if it is blessed on Friday, the day dedicated to Venus, the goddess of love and beauty. You may want to set the date for your ritual a month in advance so you have time to prepare and can target a propitious day. You must find gems and herbs that have magical frequencies in common—for example, amber and sage. One way to ensure this is to use gems and herbs associated with the same deity, like Venus. This is true for all kinds of rituals and spells, not just for charm bags.

Once you have chosen the day and time for your ritual, the rest is easy. There are many rituals and ceremonies for blessing crystals and gemstones. You can even bless more than one at a time, as long as you do it with respect for the ritual and for the spirits present. Just be sure to perform all the blessings separately; don't mix gems for one ritual with gems for another.

Today, movies and television have led us to believe that all spells and consecrations require elaborate or arcane incantations to be effective. But these are really only necessary for invoking different forms of magic. When blessing gems and stones, you don't need to say anything out loud, because these rituals are simply for balancing the powers that already exist in the stones and charging them to work in your favor. If you feel more comfortable saying an incantation, however, you can certainly do that without negatively effecting the ritual.

Once a gemstone has been blessed, keep it on your altar or in a charm bag. You can also wear it as a pendant on a chain, set it in a ring, or use it in any other type of jewelry. If you do this, be sure that you have the stone set in the piece of jewelry by a professional *before* you perform the blessing. Store the piece of jewelry in your charm bag and only take it out to wear it. This will ensure that the gemstone is not manipulated or used by someone else who may damage the energetic vibration of the stone.

Ritual to Charge Crystals and Gemstones

First, wash the stones with water (preferably river water) and a few drops of essential oil of rosemary or cinnamon, or musk oil. Clean and polish the crystals and gems with a dry handkerchief or a hand towel that you use only for this purpose. Light a candle of a color that corresponds to the gem and its magical purpose (see appendix E), and carefully pass the gemstone several times through the flame of the candle. Remember, it is important to make sure that you are not interrupted during your ritual.

Magical Properties of Crystals and Gemstones

Here is a list of gemstones and crystals commonly used in charm bags, along with their magical properties.

- *Agate*: the stone of good fortune and health; considered a type of quartz or chalcedony; loaded with high vibrations to strengthen the spirit, willpower, and decisionmaking. Absorbs negativity in any situation and nullifies envy. A piece of agate in your purse or wallet keeps away jealousy and envy; a piece under your pillow protects your dreams. Worn as a necklace or bracelet, it balances the aura and your energy.

- *Alexandrite*: the stone of the masters; occurs in a variety of colors. A gem of intellectual power that strengthens the mind and intelligence; helps you make decisions and develops the senses. Worn as a necklace, it helps bring mental clarity in studies and academic exams.

- *Amazonite*: the gem of messengers; rare gem with the power to suppress fear, balance personality, develop the senses, and strengthen the nervous system. Often used to soothe lower back pain. A piece of amazonite under the bed keeps away nightmares; hung as a pendant in a vehicle, it prevents accidents; worn as jewelry, it promotes creative expression and calms the nerves.

- *Amber*: the gem of witches; fossilized tree sap that takes on a golden color; also known as the stone of balance. It has the power to grant clairvoyance and strengthens the third eye; widely used in divination and precognition. A piece of amber grants you the favor of the spirits and fairies of the forest; in your pocket, it brings good luck and good fortune; worn as a pendant, it brings the respect of the dead. A carved amber sphere on your altar lets you see the future.

- *Amblygonite*: calms the nerves, fears, and anxiety; highly recommended for very fearful children. Placed on your altar, it prevents your fears from coming true.

- *Amethyst*: one of the gems used most in white magic; strengthens all kinds of spells, balances magical powers, calms the mind, and transmutes negative energy into positive. It is the gem of change. Commonly used for spells related to friendship, balance, wisdom, humility, and energy regeneration. Kept in your bedroom, it gives you astral vision; on your altar, it brings the favor of the spirits and strengthens divination.

- *Ametryn*: the stone of the chameleon; for those making drastic changes in their lives—moving, changing religion, changing gender, changing profession, or even making personal changes like marriage. Makes change easier; gives peace of mind so you can make decisions wisely and have the courage to face the results. Placed in the home, it facilitates favorable changes in life and in the workplace.

- *Analcime*: the health stone; used in Western white magic for its curative qualities; heals any ailment or condition. Placed in the home, it prevents diseases and ailments.

- *Andalusite*: the stone of the brave and gem of the warrior; replenishes energies and physical strength, grants health and welfare, and makes you forget your fears. In a charm bag, it grants the courage to stand your ground against any situation, however difficult it may seem.

- *Anglesite*: the quiet stone; reduces anger and bad temper; helps those who carry it stay calm and serene. Helps you override aspects of your own personality that you want to change.

- *Ankerite*: gem dedicated to Eros and Aphrodite, the primordial gods of love. Grants loyalty, love, confidence, and willpower to continue any relationship; attracts love and passion for life. Add to a charm bag to help you find your soul mate. A piece submerged in pure honey for nine nights brings back a lover who has left.

- *Apatite*: reduces anger, appeases rage, and promotes harmony; has soothing powers, especially on children. A piece of apatite hanging from a silver chain reduces hyperactivity in infants; hung at the end of the bed, it brings pleasant dreams.

- **Apophyllite**: the healing gem; has strong affinity to the powers of Air; believed to help prevent hurricanes and storms. Commonly used to heal congenital illnesses or rare inherited conditions. Helps you listen to your instincts so you make better decisions.

- **Aquamarine**: the gem of sailors; widely used to prevent seasickness; grants the favor of sea creatures and spirits of the West. Prevents shipwrecks and getting lost at sea. Worn as a necklace, it protects against drowning; worn as a bracelet, it promotes peace of mind, meditation, and spirituality.

- **Aragonite**: helps you relate to a group or to people close to you; related to friendship and humility; often used by the children of witches from a young age to achieve lasting friendships. Carried in a wallet, it attracts new business proposals; worn as a pendant, it attracts many friends.

- **Atacamite**: attractive green stone that strengthens protective magic and psychic defenses, as well as all kinds of rituals to ward off negative entities. Recommended in treatment of mental patients and people with mental weakness. Placed for a few minutes on the forehead, it calms headaches, nausea, and dizziness.

- **Aventurine**: a form of quartz that influences the feelings; a good gift for artists, writers, philosophers, and thinkers as it strengthens concentration and creativity and wards off distractions. Worn as a necklace, it balances thoughts and keeps you focused on your goals, clearing obstacles and distractions from your path.

The Magical Art of Crafting Charm Bags

- *Axinite*: a very rare gem that symbolizes progress, prosperity, and evolution; promotes success in a profession or successful achievement of a long-term goal; assures success in legal proceedings. Widely used by seers and psychics to perform regressions and quick visits to the past. Placed on your altar, it allows you to visit your past lives and grants you the gift of visualizing previous mistakes.

- *Azurite*: the gem of memory and mementos, associated with the gods of thought and wisdom. Strengthens the mind and especially memory; commonly used by witches in spells to regain memories or combat amnesia. Given as a gift, it calms excessive delusions of grandeur or vanity and fights stress.

- *Baryte (barite)*: pearlescent mineral available in many colors, associated with confidence and self-esteem; promotes concentration and combats sleeplessness. Under your pillow, it fights insomnia; worn on a chain around your neck, it cancels out envy and jealousy toward others.

- *Beryllium*: suitable for all kinds of meditation and very good for developing concentration and intuitive powers; commonly used in séances, yoga, and meditation. Recommended for young students with concentration problems who are not able to process information correctly.

- *Bixbite (red beryllium, red emerald)*: a peculiar mineral with the power to manipulate, create, perceive, or influence all kinds of emotions in living beings. Grants witches and sorcerers the power to influence other people's emotions and dispel negative thoughts.

- *Blende*: used in ancient times to protect against accidents and disasters related to forces of Nature; currently used in rituals to prevent earthquakes and storms and to ward off lightning and hurricanes; associated with wind power. Placed on the roof of a house, it wards off lightning and protects from thunderstorms; hung from the helm of a ship, it protects against wrecks; hung in a car, it prevents accidents.

- **Blood jasper**: a variety similar to leopard jasper, the proper gem to fight feelings of negativity, depression, melancholy, or sadness.

- **Blue agate**: has great powers of purification; use to balance time in your favor and to balance your emotions.

- **Bornite**: associated with cancer and regressive diseases; difficult to find and only recommended for sorcerers and shamans with expert knowledge of its power. In a cloth bag, it decreases the discomfort associated with various medical conditions.

- **Brown agate**: brings balance and equilibrium to your life and puts your feet back on the ground.

- **Calcite**: formerly used by Arabs to bring peace to the home; a purifying and decorative gem with the ability to override all the negativity around it. Keep lots of it in your home. Placed in the corner of a room, it wards off nightmares; strategically placed in each corner of a house, it prevents fights and arguments.

- **Carnelian**: a variety of red agate best known as the gem of spontaneity; commonly used in rituals associated with health. Recommended as jewelry for the elderly or for those suffering from chronic ailments; brings health, happiness, and protection to those who wear it. Carried during meditation, it opens your mind to other planes of existence and gives you (with practice) the ability to call and make contact with souls.

- **Cassiterite**: attractive gem that strengthens all feelings, positive or negative; has special powers over lovers; widely used in rituals that affect the will of the people. Carried during meditation and yoga sessions, it opens and strengthens the chakras, stimulates positive thoughts, and balances the aura.

- **Cat's eye**: usually found in shades of green and yellow; related to inner peace, calm, serenity, and spiritual balance; attracts good omens and prophetic dreams. Worn as an amulet during meditation, it promotes concentration and peace of mind; hung from a bedroom window, it attracts happiness and calm and dispels evil spirits. Not to be confused with Alexandrite, sometimes also called cat's eye.

- **Celestine**: overrides fears and self-imposed obstacles; helps you release and express creativity. Widely used by artists and comedians, as it helps project the joy in their work; helps them gain confidence and shed fears. Worn as a ring, it calms and dissipates headaches and migraines; helps you better understand your talents and weaknesses and better express your various faculties.

- **Cerussite**: associated with the heart organ and its chakra. Its vibration is related to healing and blood circulation; widely used for treatments associated with veins. Worn around the neck, it calms and balances the nervous system, cleanses the blood, and decreases heart disease.

- **Chalcedony**: powerful gem of protection with special powers to protect your loved ones; absorbs negative energy and purifies evil; prevents betrayal and warns of enemies around you. A gem of high energy. Washing every Thursday with rose water increases its power.

- *Chalcopyrite*: ore with a metallic sheen closely associated with health; has positive powers over all fields of medicine. Washed in river water, it improves health and strengthens the effects of natural medicines and treatments; worn as a necklace, it significantly prolongs life and improves health.

- *Charoita*: translucent mineral with shades between lavender and purple; use to block negativity, fear, and enemy actions; wards off deep fears and increases the positive energy of all individuals. Placed on your altar, it keeps the energies clean and stable, balances the forces of magic, and dispels any obstacles in your path.

- *Chrysoberyl*: green translucent mineral more like a gem that promotes positive energy; commonly used by witches who perform magic with the Fire element. Carried in your purse, it keeps you solvent and calm at all times; placed on an altar, it helps with meditation.

- *Cinnabar*: deep red stone with powers bound to love, passion, intensity, and sexuality, as well as blood and the circulatory system; effective in all healing rituals related to blood circulation. Placed in a red cloth sack, it improves blood circulation and cleanses the circulatory system; given as a gift to a couple, it ensures many offspring.

- *Citrine*: gem of the Sun, happiness, and abundance; commonly used for rituals in which the solar powers of the gods are invoked. Gives great energy to the wearer; helps to develop creativity and intellect; fights stress and fear; strengthens spiritual powers. Carried daily, it promotes creativity, joy, and enthusiasm; also used in rituals of high magic to invoke the favor of the Sun gods.

- **Coral**: gem of power and protection *par excellence*, strongly recommended for police, military members, and fighters; protects and guards against evil. Worn as an amulet, it provides security and willpower; placed in the collars and apparel of pets, it protects them from poisoning and accidents.

- **Danburite**: native to Tanzania; related to the intellect and imagination. Its powers are associated with neuronal capacity. An egg-shaped piece placed as a table centerpiece attracts prosperity and joy to the home.

- **Diamond**: the stone of kings; strengthens the capacity to perform magic and all sorts of spells and magical rituals. Its power is linked to light. Use with great care, because it has the unusual quality of awakening negative thoughts, as well as vanity and treachery. Attracts prosperity and success, prolongs life, and promotes all forms of positive and negative magic.

- **Dioptase**: little-known mineral with the power to absorb personal pain, make you forget sad or painful times, and even erase all kinds of trauma and undesirable experiences. Carrying a piece of dioptase for a long time may help you overcome all kinds of trauma and bad memories.

- **Dolomite**: natural calcium-and-magnesium-based carbonate with the power to calm tempers and ward off all negative or evil entities; use in spells that locate or track evil or negativity. Carried in your purse or wallet, it warns you when something negative is about to happen, or when you must not trust someone who plans to betray you.

- **Dumortierite**: the gem of hope, commonly used in the manufacture of fine porcelain; often confused with lapis lazuli. This gem in any form fights depression, promotes joy, and gives hope to its wearer. Worn as a bracelet or medallion, it gives hope and courage to face any situation.

- **Emerald**: the gem of balance, has the power of purification; dissipates all kinds of obstacles and fears; balances your time and your life. From antiquity, it has been credited with the ability to neutralize poisons and improve sight. Worn as jewelry, it improves health and prolongs life; carried as an amulet, it brings good luck and removes every obstacle from your path.

- **Epidote**: associated with the magic of forests, Nature, and the Earth; use in rituals to strengthen the symbolic and material structure of the home, prevent earthquakes, and conjure up the spirits of the land. Placed in a blue felt bag, it relaxes the nervous system; in a green cloth bag, it increases clairvoyance.

- **Fluorite**: very attractive gem that helps develop memory; widely used in spells to attract love, enthusiasm, and reconciliation with individuals from the past. Placed in a room, it brings harmony and peace; carried during meditation, it recovers the balance between body, mind, and spirit.

- **Galena**: gray lead-colored mineral associated with harmony between the different planes of existence and the balance of body and soul; gives spontaneity to its wearer. Often used to improve memory and combat short-term amnesia. Carried in a cloth bag, it brings you spontaneity to speak in public and interact with others.

- **Garnet**: known as the gem of the immortal; according to folklore, it has the unique power to delay aging and prolong the life of the wearer. Widely used in spells and rituals associated with understanding, confidence, creativity, perception, and sincerity. Placed on your altar, it grants you the favor of spirits and extends the power of all your spells.

- **Gold**: known as the "metal of kings." Has qualities to attract happiness and protection; use in rituals to bring abundance and wealth. A gold piece on your altar is essential to conjuring success and job promotions; also known for its protective powers.

- **Green agate**: commonly used to build self-esteem and override depression; helps you get to the root of a problem.

- **Green quartz (prasiolite)**: used in white magic to attract prosperity, wealth, and good fortune; related to the magic of goblins and forest spirits.

- **Hawk's eye**: has a peculiar greenish color; commonly used by the greatest clairvoyants between 1920 and 1950. In combination with cat's eye, it makes a powerful amulet to strengthen mental shields and develop extrasensory abilities. Placed on the forehead, it stimulates the third-eye chakra and develops spiritual vision.

- **Heliotrope**: known for its healing powers; a very good choice for healing rituals of the blood and for brief meditations. Placed in your home, it creates an atmosphere of quite pleasant harmony; also very suitable for self-healing rituals.

- **Hematite**: widely used in protective magic as an energy shield; raises the mystical aura and strengthens spells and rituals of protection; decreases negativity and the strength of hexes against you. Worn around the neck during meditation, it strengthens your psyche and your ability to concentrate, as well as your astral energy fields.

- *Hessonite*: reddish-brown garnet linked to the achievement of goals and objectives; promotes positive changes and attracts success, prosperity, and joy. Placed in a red cloth sachet, it provides good fortune and improves life in all its aspects.

- *Iolite (cordierite)*: rare gem used in jewelry for its hardness and bright color; intimately linked to the magic of the planet Saturn. Protects its wearer from negative energy; brings fortune, health, good reputation, and wealth. Worn as jewelry on a Saturday (Saturn day), it protects the wearer from negativity, spells, and incantations.

- *Jacinto quartz*: blood-red quartz widely used in rituals and charms to bring good luck and better fortune. Worn as jewelry, it protects against envy, jealousy, and bad vibrations; placed as an ornament on a high surface in a house, it wards off bad energy and promotes success in all projects.

- *Jade*: commonly used in rituals to bring stability, fortune, and good luck; widely used in white magic to balance karma and energy vibes. Purifies and strengthens positive energies and gives extra energy to any charm or ritual for prosperity.

- *Jasper*: protection gem *par excellence*; widely used by Native Americans in rituals to conjure the Great Spirits and the older gods; particularly associated with spirituality and auspiciousness. Worn as an amulet, it promotes honest friendships, willpower, patience, and perseverance; placed on your altar, it grants the favor of the spirits in your rituals.

- *Jet*: known for its high spiritual and magical vibrations; widely used in magic related to protection and spiritual defense. This is the perfect gem to combat the Evil Eye and envy; children often wear bracelets containing jet to ward off evil. Worn around the neck, it protects you from envy and professional jealousy.

- **Kunzite**: transparent, pink-streaked mineral associated with love and protection; dispels negative energies in the environment and completely overrides sadness. Placed in a home, it calms the mind and nervous system, and brings peace, love, and joy to the environment; given to high-energy people, it induces calm.

- **Kyanite**: widely used in jewelry to bring good luck and attract love; dispels doubts and helps young people in their search for love. Placed in a vase full of roses, it attracts love and brings steadfastness in a relationship; worn as jewelry, it attracts good luck; given as a gift, it promises good fortune and a lasting friendship.

- **Labradorite**: blue-green stone that dispels uncertainties and trauma; recommended to improve self-esteem and personal security; increases creativity and gives courage to carry out any project. Carried during working meetings, it decreases stress and nervous breakdowns.

- **Lapis lazuli**: attractive gemstone of blue, silver, or gold that strengthens intuition and mental communication; promotes telepathy and empathy. Used by the Egyptians to neutralize poisons, today it is used in talismans that strengthen powers and protect against psychic attacks. Attracts fame, success, and good fortune and dispels negative thoughts and obstacles.

- **Larimar (pectolite)**: best known as "the blue stone"; promotes calm and creativity, as well as the desire to carry out all projects. Commonly used in healing magic and rituals that nourish the body and mind; used to ease the pain of frequent headaches. Carried in a portfolio, it helps you positively accept sudden changes and adapt to them better; also helps refurbish your own energies.

- **Leopard-skin jasper**: associated with karma, equilibrium, and balance; commonly used in yoga and *tai chi* to balance the mind, body, and spirit; also harmonizes the chakras and aura hues. This is a gem of absolute equilibrium. Worn around the neck, it gives you emotional balance.

- **Lilac agate**: for everything related to the arts, especially poetry, music, and painting.

- **Magnesite (calcium carbonate)**: develops spirituality and magic with water. According to folklore, it was used with sea-water and nacre shells to conjure water spirits.

- **Magnetite (magnet rock)**: known for its strong electromagnetic qualities; commonly associated with magic to balance, attract, and send out forces; use to strengthen healing and avoid distractions. Place it by the front door of a house to balance energies and reduce unwanted visits; keeps away troublemakers.

- **Malachite**: widely used against the Evil Eye, envy, and bad thoughts; also commonly used by magicians since ancient times to cleanse the blood and strengthen medical treatments. Place it in a table centerpiece to encourage creativity, relaxation, inspiration, and intelligence.

- **Marcasite**: commonly used in healing magic to reduce aches and pains; increasingly used for alleviating the problems of renal calculi and kidney stones. Soaked in herbal oil every dawn and placed behind a door, it attracts health and good luck.

- *Milky quartz*: strongly recommended for those with medical conditions related to the nervous system, and especially those who suffer from depression or nervous breakdowns.

- *Moldavite*: rare gem energetically linked to the nerves and moods; attracts calm and tranquility, dissipates stillness, and awakens the mind. Recommended for those suffering from nervous breakdowns or anxiety; relaxes thoughts and gently calms the emotions.

- *Montana moss agate*: stained gem found in North America with the power to cleanse spaces and auras from negative entities or spells.

- *Moonstone*: commonly associated with femininity and nighttime magic; soothes fears and bad thoughts; balances the emotions and calms your enemies. Commonly used in rituals and spells to make women regain lost fertility. A moonstone strengthens altar magic and incantations related to the wind, nighttime, and water.

- *Moss agate*: gem of protection *par excellence*; good gift for people who are prone to accidents.

- *Mother of pearl (nacre)*: associated with the magic of Venus and the female divinities; usually worn by women to highlight their feminine attractiveness and for dominance in work situations; strengthens all forms of femininity and spells performed by women. Also widely used by priestesses in conjunction with pearls and coral to reinforce the magic of their charms. Hung from the neck, it gives you the blessing of warrior goddesses; worn as other jewelry, it brings out your natural beauty.

- *Obsidian*: protective stone with high vibrations of light that dissipate negativity, spells, and bad thoughts; protects against witchcraft and mental attacks and promotes meditation and spiritual balance. Placed under the bed, it protects you from psychic attacks and spells while you rest; also protects your dreams and keeps your projects from being impeded.

- *Olivine*: complement to spells and rituals that attract joy and prosperity; protects against bad luck and misfortune. Present it to your beloved so that he or she always thinks of you. This is a good energy cleanser, effective against all kinds of bad karma and spiritual discomfort.

- *Onyx*: symbolizes freedom and optimism; often used to override feelings of sadness or depression; reflects back on others everything they wished for you—positive or negative; also reflects feelings and dreams in the earthly plane. Worn as an amulet, it protects against all misfortunes and accidents; use to ward off evil thoughts.

- *Opal*: gem found in a wide range of colors that can be linked to different shades of the aura and thus stimulate different powers, according to your specific needs. Carried as an amulet or worn as jewelry, it provides serenity, calm, patience, and spiritual development; dispels fears.

- *Orange agate*: opens the mind and strengthens creativity, imagination, and curiosity.

- *Ox eye*: usually reddish brown in color with golden hues; linked to physical capacities and the development of strength, endurance, and skill; good luck for sportsmen and athletes. Worn as a necklace or pendant close to the chest, it protects the heart and takes care of any disease.

- *Pearl*: known since antiquity for its brilliance and hardness; symbolizes purity, innocence, and kindness; commonly used in protective white magic. Worn as jewelry, it brings honest and lasting friendships and good luck; enhances intuition.

- **Petrified (fossil) wood**: opalized wood of ancient trees with powers strongly linked to the ether, the fifth element of the pentacle. Use for spells associated with the passage of time, nullifying or impairing predestined actions and events, and strengthening the ability to perform regressions. Not often carried as an amulet or worn as jewelry because of its very high spiritual vibration.

- **Prehnite**: interesting mineral widely used in magic to resolve conflicts and personal problems; strengthens the character and fosters good relationships. Recommended for people who have difficulty with self-acceptance. A good gift for those who have some form of depression or emotional conflict, which it can help them resolve quickly.

- **Pyrite**: mineral with a high psychic vibration that strengthens the intellect as well as the aura and mental shields; widely used in meditation, homeopathic medicine, and meetings of astral projection. Placed by a door, it protects a home and its surroundings from negative psychic vibrations and keeps away ghosts.

- **Quartz**: found in a variety of colors, all with different qualities and powers; channels all kinds of energies. Commonly used to ward off evil thoughts, absorb negativity, and promote positive thoughts. Quartz in all its forms is found in the repertoire of all believers and practitioners of the old traditions; shamans and witches also make use of its many healing properties. Useful in a variety of rituals, it has the power to project all your dreams, desires, and thoughts. Place a piece of quartz in your charm bags to accelerate the projection of your wishes or make your magical powers stronger.

- **Quartz crystal**: receives, nullifies, transmits, and amplifies all kinds of energy vibrations; stimulates the creation of new energy. Strengthens meditation and concentration, empowers all other crystals, and develops patience and powers of healing.

- **Red agate (fire agate)**: arouses dormant energies and stimulates sexual energy; strengthens the soul and blesses young relationships.

- **Red jasper**: favors love and all rituals and spells with aphrodisiac intentions; influences the health of the heart and feelings of affection and friendship; attracts fidelity and everlasting love. Combined in a charm bag with a variety of herbs and flowers associated with Venus, it conjures love and passion, promotes fidelity, and strengthens relationships.

- **Rhodochrosite**: rare mineral usually found in shades of pink, red, or brown; widely used in witchcraft and folk magic to strengthen or cancel specific feelings and thoughts. Worn as jewelry, it wards against mental manipulation and helps heal emotional wounds.

- **Rhodonite**: known as the "rose stone" for its particular brightness and pink color; attracts joy, love, goodwill, and friendship. Use in magic associated with emotional and spiritual healing; also dispels the doubts of the heart and mind. Carved into a heart shape, it attracts love and fidelity.

- **Rose quartz**: stimulates positive thoughts, especially those of affection and friendship. Recommended for people with personality disorders or mental-development conditions to stimulate confidence and the feelings associated with mood and affection.

- **Ruby**: beautiful red gemstone known since antiquity as the "gem of the prophets" because of its power to attract prophetic dreams and strengthen clairvoyance during séances. Carried as an amulet, it brings good luck and confidence; worn as jewelry, it builds character and the capacity to see what is hidden in front of you.

- **Rutilated quartz**: red, black, and gold translucent variety of quartz that appears to contain internal fractures; popularly known as the "hair of the goddess Venus" for its peculiar appearance. Its power is associated with health, the regeneration of tissues, the acceleration of healing, and all types of medical treatment.

- **Rutile**: rare crystal associated with personal success and glory; helps those who set very difficult goals to achieve them; promotes peace, spontaneity, creativity, ingenuity, and meditation.

- **Sapphire**: popularly known as the "stone of merchants"; provides mental clarity and stimulates intuition and the sentiments of a couple. According to folklore, if a married couple carry sapphire rings, loyalty and happiness will always bless them. Sapphire used in any form brings patience, peace, mental health, and the wisdom to make decisions.

- **Sapphire quartz**: associated with astral magic and sorcery; strengthens enchantments carried out during major astronomical events like eclipses.

- **Sard**: the gem for those who overcome obstacles; linked to intelligence, wisdom, and creativity; calms the mind and gives peace of mind to help resolve any situation. Carried during study and meditation, it relaxes the mind, removes distractions, and strengthens concentration.

- **Sardonyx**: variety of onyx used in magic to raise personal powers and self-confidence; brings courage and humility; improves intuition and moral sense. Worn around the neck, it encourages you to be better every day and increases morale and happiness.

- **Selenite**: translucent form of crystallized gypsum known in European folklore as "the crystal of angels" or "lunar crystals"; promotes happiness at home and encourages creativity as well as joy and good luck. It is often placed on an altar and used in rituals to attract lunar energy or to win the favor of celestial beings and reveal their secrets.

- **Serpentine**: relieves physical and emotional pain; use in various magical rituals to strengthen the body and prevent disease. A piece shaped as a medallion relieves constant headaches and muscle aches; use as a decoration to prevent accidents to family members.

- **Silver**: linked to lunar magic and rituals of protection in white magic and shamanism. In folklore, frequently used to generate prophetic dreams and develop mental communication. Silver in any form wards off evil and has the power to strengthen magic that is performed at night.

- **Smoky quartz**: variety of quartz with yellow-smoked colors; the national stone of Scotland. Relieves tension, fear, and inner fears; combats all kinds of personal frustration, negativity, and pessimism. Use in relaxation sessions and to stimulate health.

- **Soapstone**: stone of constancy that symbolizes love, purity, success, and perseverance. Also known as the protective stone of the trader because of its ability to promote the success of a business and protect its owners. Placed near the entrance to a business, it attracts good sales and protection; worn as jewelry or on a key chain, it prevents physical and mental exhaustion.

- **Sodalite**: gemstone most often used in holistic healing therapies to balance the chakras, the aura, and all energy points of the body and mind. Encourages humility. Worn as jewelry, it helps control nerves and cultivate creativity, good speech, and spontaneity.

- **Sphalerite**: associated with health and balance; strengthens immunity and heals all diseases and delicate health conditions. Worn as a collar, it cures ailments, stops bleeding, and prevents poisonings.

- **Sphene (titanite)**: inspires adventurers to fulfill their dreams and meet their goals; protects travelers and stimulates creativity; resolves all kinds of conflicts. Hung from the bedside, it motivates you to stick with your goals and not give up; also recommended for dreamers and travelers.

- **Spinel**: gem of high society; a ruby-like mineral associated with greatness and success; promotes working people from one position to another. Worn as a ring, it symbolizes leadership and facilitates a rapid ascent.

- **Sugilite**: associated with intelligence, calm, and emotional balance; recommended to dissipate stress and distractions. Also used to cancel negative thoughts. Use as decoration or wear as jewelry to eliminate all kinds of negative entities, remove obstacles, and calm the mind; place it under a pillow to give rest and restore energy.

- **Sunstone**: known for its strong link with masculinity and magic performed during the day; gives courage and character, balances the mind, and strengthens physical skills. Used by shamans to make contact with the Earth and the Sun. A sunstone strengthens altar spells and rituals associated with elemental Fire, Earth, day, and prosperity.

- *Tiger's eye*: known as the gem that makes witches immortal; prolongs life and youth, restores health, and cleanses and balances karma. Commonly used in rituals to ward off messengers of death. Placed under a pillow, it helps you visualize future events in a dream. This gem has the ability to get lost and always return to its owner.

- *Topaz*: symbolizes friendship and balance, as well as teamwork; commonly used to strengthen intuition and intellect. Use in magic to protect large sites, land, and farms from negative entities and thieves. Worn as jewelry, it helps develop psychic abilities and astral travel; blue topaz establishes new links with other worlds.

- *Tourmaline*: "stone of the energies," known for its virtues in magic and witchcraft. Use to strengthen all sorts of positive rituals and talismans that protect from evil; balances energies and neutralizes enemies on sight. Worn as a pendant or necklace, it stimulates the growth of magical powers; worn as a ring, it decreases vices.

- *Turquoise*: prolongs life and gives a peaceful and dignified death; removes the ailments of old age; promotes skin health and well-being in many ways. Turquoise used in any form, either as jewelry, ornaments, or on ceremonial garments, attracts and stimulates very positive energy.

- *Unakite*: uncommon form of speckled granite in shades from green to red; strengthens all virtues in general; use in rituals that stimulate specific aspects of personality. A piece cut and polished in the shape of your favorite animal protects you as a guardian spirit would; carved in the shape of an egg, it attracts wealth, love, and success.

- **Variscite**: strengthens intuition and memory; wards off psychic attacks and spells, as well as magic potions that negatively influence feelings. Placed under a pillow, it cures insomnia; worn as jewelry, it promotes virility and fertility.

- **Yellow agate**: has power over health; highly recommended for upset stomachs.

- **Zirconium**: best known as zircon, this gem is widely used in seership; associated with meditation and clairvoyance. Commonly used in rituals to invoke prosperity, happiness, and protection. Placed on the forehead for several minutes every day, it helps develop clairvoyance and allows a clear view of the future.

- **Zoisite**: commonly used to fight feelings of envy and to dissipate jealousy; also very strong in the area of health, balancing it and providing strong support to the immune system. Relieves aches and general discomfort. Carried in your bag, it heals you physically and emotionally. It is the right gem to combat depressive states.

Chapter 10

Using Oils and Essences in Charm Bags

Fragrances have enormous power. They can inspire love or easily disenchant someone. Perfumes, creams, and aromatic oils all share the same powers. In fact, an exquisite fragrance can be your signature wherever you go, while a faint scent that encourages a positive reaction before an interview can assure your success. A lingering hint of your fragrance when you leave can make sure everyone wants you to return soon. That is, of course, if you know how to choose the right fragrance.

When you use fragrances to consecrate talismans—and especially charm bags—you give them that same power. Just by spraying a few drops of aromatic essential oil on a charm bag, or by anointing the gems and herbs with oil before introducing them into the bag, you can endow it with all the energies of that essence.

The world of essential oils is extremely complex and wide-ranging. In this chapter, we will look at a fairly short list of oils that have widely diverse magical uses. I have some practical knowledge of these oils and have worked with them for some time in homeopathic medicine, so I have great confidence in their powers.

Most of the oils listed below can be bought in specialty shops. But with the right guidance, you can also learn to produce them yourself in the comfort of your home. You can learn to customize essential oils for many different uses, ranging from simple aromatherapy to elaborate rituals and alternative treatments. Aromatherapy, homeopathic medicine, and naturopathic perfumery all draw on the magical associations and diverse qualities of different natural and essential oils, and you can make use of those properties for either medicinal or spiritual purposes. Bach flower therapy, grounded in the work of physician Edward Bach, and the studies of herbal researchers are all linked to the magical powers and associations of fragrances and essential oils.

Here, we will look at the magical and spiritual properties of various vegetable oils—high-fat oils that are usually extracted by pressure from various plants like sunflowers, poppy, and walnuts. Vegetable oils have nourishing and regenerative properties for the skin, as well as a high vitamin content. That is part of the reason why they are used in alternative medicine and natural beauty treatments. Common vegetable oils include sweet almond oil, rosehip oil, and olive oil, which are important ingredients in cooking because of their multiple attributes that support health.

In addition, we will look at essential oils that, unlike vegetable oils, are generally derived by distilling different parts (flowers, leaves, seeds, etc.) of plants, shrubs, and trees. These include aromatic oils like jasmine, myrrh, and vetiver. Essential oils are often used for therapeutic purposes and also for perfumes. They are generally useful as antiseptics, painkillers, and immuno-stimulants. In most cases, these essential oils should be mixed with other vegetable oils or with milk, because, in concentrated doses, they can be irritants and harmful to the body.

Some essential oils have aphrodisiac properties, like cinnamon, jasmine, ginger, and rose. Other oils, like basil, eucalyptus, and mint, are known stimulants for the mind and for mental development. Some oils are relaxing or soothing, like cedar oil, and some are anti-depressant, like bergamot, patchouli, and neroli. Generally speaking, there are six different groups of essential oils, each with their own specific properties and purposes:

- **Citrus oils**: These bring vitality, energy, courage, and optimism, and have a fresh fragrance full of character. Examples are lemon and bergamot.

- **Herbal oils**: These promote concentration, strength, and character; they dispel doubts and increase self-esteem. Examples are vetiver, citronella, and eucalyptus.

- **Resinous oils**: These are formed by cellular secretion and have a strong connection with the spirit; they attract balance and freedom. Examples are amber, myrrh, and storax.

- **Woody oils**: These promote strength, inner calm, spiritual strength, and protection. Examples are sandalwood, cedar, and cypress.

- **Exotic floral oils**: These tend to be inspiring, energizing, captivating, and sedative. Examples are ylang ylang, neroli, and orchid.

- **Wild floral oils**: These bring happiness and courage, and help develop the spirit and personality. Examples are chamomile, thyme, and lemon verbena.

These oils are natural allies for you that can enhance your life in various ways. Since they are extracted from various parts of plants, they retain the healing and beneficial properties of the plants, as well as part of their magical spirit. This allows them to empower and complement your spells and charm bags.

I recommend that, as you begin to work with essential oils, you purchase them in a specialty shop or boutique. Practice using these oils to consecrate your charm bags. As you advance in practice, you can acquire new fragrances, combine fragrances, or even create your own oils. Eventually, you will have a full range of essential oils in your home to support your various purposes, whether magical or therapeutic.

Magical Properties of Oils and Essences

Here is a summary of the essential and vegetable oils most commonly used in charm bags and rituals.

- *Agrimonia*: Also known as "grass of San Guillermo," this beneficent essential oil is distilled from the tiny yellow flowers of the plant. Agrimonia is highly regarded for its various medicinal qualities. In ancient times, it was used as an infusion to treat infections of the liver. It is a strong astringent, a tonic, a diuretic, and a decongestant for the digestive system. According to European folklore, its flowers warn when evil is near; in medicine, it is used to treat jaundice and infections of the tonsils. In Bach flower therapy and herbal sorcery, it is used to dispel anguish and harmful emotions, dissipate stress caused by constant worries, and combat the tendency to fall into various addictions. Add some flowers or a few drops of the essential oil to charm bags to strengthen joy, happiness, and relaxation, and to dissipate constant stress or fight your inner fears.

- *Angelica (Angelica archangelica)*: In Catholic tradition, this plant was a gift from the Archangel Gabriel and is also known as "holy spirit weed." The essential oil has strong medicinal properties. It is a strong aperitif, a digestive, an anti-microbial, an expectorant, and a sedative. In homeopathic medicine, it is used to treat insomnia, gastroenteritis, bronchitis, asthma, migraines, and some ulcers. Despite all these healing properties, contact with the oil at very high concentrations or in high dosage may result in respiratory allergies that paralyze the nervous system, and may produce dermatitis. Essential oil of angelica is often used in certain forms of spiritualism, shamanism, and European Voodoo to conjure spirits from beyond the grave or to dominate them. Use it to consecrate images for protective purposes and for charm bags that strengthen clairvoyance, spirituality, and all links with divinity.

• *Anise*: Often used to treat cramps and various digestive disorders and stomach ailments, this oil, which is distilled from the seeds, is also used to treat dry cough and other symptoms associated with influenza because it is a powerful expectorant. In white magic and witchcraft, anise oil is commonly used to soothe headaches and nausea, relieve anxiety, cure insomnia, and as a strong aphrodisiac. It is used to complement many spells and rituals associated with increasing loving attraction and sexual passion. Use a few drops of essential oil of anise seeds to consecrate charm bags intended for aphrodisiac and loving purposes. In combination with rosemary oil, it is an excellent magnet for good luck.

• *Basil*: This oil is used in homeopathy and aromatherapy to provide relief and balance to the body and to restore inner calm and reach a state of complete peace. It is also used in perfumery and aromatherapy as a base to mix with other oils for homeopathic purposes and to develop certain cures and more specific treatments against stress and annoyance caused by routine. Apply a few drops to charm bags intended to give you inner calm and peace of mind.

• *Benzoin*: An aromatic plant extract used to ward off negative thoughts and avoid being influenced by them, it is also commonly used by witches to perfume objects to prevent them from being possessed by spirits and external forces. It is an anti-inflammatory, anti-oxidant, and expectorant, and is used in magic and sorcery to dispel grief and keep away enemies. Add a few drops to charm bags to strengthen clairvoyance and spiritual protection. You can also use it to consecrate a little bag full of dried roots of rosemary and sage to strengthen your divination sessions.

- **Bergamot**: Oil extracted from bergamot bark is widely used in the world of perfumery to develop fragrances with both male and female character. In alternative medicine, it is used to calm anxiety, relieve depression, and dispel sadness. In magic, it is commonly used to protect against fear of the unknown and other fears. Amulets devoted to gods and warriors were often anointed with it. It is also used in white magic to fight sadness and depression, and for anointing candles and magical tools. According to popular belief, blessing amulets and jewelry with bergamot oil attracts and promotes positivism and joy, as well as friendship. In Hoodoo, it was used to control, direct, and dominate others. Use it to anoint charm bags to positively affect moods, instill confidence and courage, improve attitudes, and attract prosperity.

- **Birch**: The essential oil distilled from birch bark is widely used in aromatherapy and in the world of holistic medicine as a natural sedative and muscle relaxant. It is also used to heal shallow wounds and skin rashes. It is commonly used to anoint or "dress" certain talismans, amulets, or images associated with renewal, rebirth, love, and spiritual strength. Anointing the doors of a house with birch oil frightens away evil spirits, demons, and ghosts. Images and totems anointed with birch oil ward off evil spirits, and talismans consecrated with it are used to accompany exorcisms. Use a few drops to anoint gems, herbs, and other items contained in a charm bag to combat evil, and to ward off evil thoughts, hexes, and malicious spirits.

- **Cedar**: Known for its properties to promote concentration, cedar provides relaxation while meditating and reduces stress, thanks to its relaxing and refreshing fragrance. Cedar oil was used in ancient Egypt as a special blend with other ingredients to embalm mummies because it was long lasting and because it lessened unpleasant organic odors. In ancient Greece, it was considered, along with laurel, cypress, and myrtle, to be one of the most appropriate oils for honoring the deities in their temples. In white magic and certain forms of witchcraft, it is used to bless and consecrate all kinds of magical tools and to scare away evil spirits. Anoint five blue or indigo candles with oil of cedar and cypress and light them next to "the window that faces north" so that spirits stay away permanently. Use a few drops to anoint charm bags to protect and exorcize evil.

- **Chamomile**: This essential oil, which is extracted from the flower, is not very common in many countries, despite the fact that chamomile flowers are well known and widely used as a natural relaxant and daily digestive. It is a natural anti-inflammatory, an antiseptic, a digestive, and a sedative analgesic. In homeopathy and Bach flower treatments, it is commonly used as a powerful relaxant and anti-depressant. It is also used as an infusion to combat conjunctivitis, migraine, heartburn, and insomnia. In white magic, chamomile flowers, like their oil, are used in rituals that channel the healing energies of the Earth and to bless talismans to bring peace and rest to others. In Spain and Germany, modern witches bless decorative gems with a few drops of this essential oil to attract peace and quiet. Use it to consecrate charm bags dedicated to that purpose.

- **Cinnamon**: One of the most recognized oils, cinnamon is renowned for its versatility. It is used in pharmaceutical, homeopathic, and naturopathic treatments, in perfumes, and even in gastronomy. The essential oil extracted from the bark is highly aphrodisiac, relaxing, sedative, and antiseptic. It strengthens the immune system by providing energy to the body's natural defenses and is a good local stimulant. Cinnamon and its oil are both widely used in various forms of magic and witchcraft to attract protection and foresight, as well as to strengthen all kinds of spells. Burn cinnamon sticks on your altar to bring good luck; carry a stick in your wallet to prevent you from running out of money. Use the essential oil to bless and consecrate charm bags with aphrodisiac, mental, or protective character.

- *Clove*: A plant native to Indonesia; commonly used in cooking and gastronomy, and, in certain countries, to manufacture cigarettes and aromatic jewelry; also used in homeopathic medicine, aromatherapy, and in various holistic therapies. Gargling with an infusion of clove is said to decrease toothache significantly. Clove is naturally anesthetic and anti-inflammatory, and has anti-bacterial properties. In homeopathic medicine—as well as in Traditional Chinese Medicine and Tibetan medicine—the essential oil is used as a powerful local anesthetic and anti-inflammatory, while in aromatherapy it is used to provide calm, relaxing, and warm stimulation to the patient. The essential oil is used in witchcraft to consecrate amulets and jewelry given as gifts of protection. It is a powerful aphrodisiac and stimulates loving emotions. Use it to consecrate protective charm bags or those designed to stimulate love and passion.

- *Coriander*: The aromatic oil extracted from the seeds of coriander is a strong paliative for the mind and spirit. It helps fight stress, tension, and negative thoughts, and is used to consecrate talismans of protection and to ease fears. Its strong positive charge raises self-esteem, promotes ingenuity and creativity, and helps engender more positive attitudes. Add a few drops to charm bags to promote positivism and joy.

- **Cypress**: This essential oil is commonly used as a sedative and natural relaxant. The oil, which is extracted from various parts of the plant, emits a scent similar to that of cedar. It has a strong fragrance and great character, but is also relaxing, which is why it is used to perfume and deodorize all kinds of environments and closed spaces. It is naturally astringent, anti-spasmodic, anti-perspirant, anti-rheumatic, antiseptic, and healing. In homeopathic medicine, it is used to reduce cellulite, open varicose veins, and fight fluid retention. In aromatherapy, it is used to provide calm and tranquility to people following a brief treatment. In popular culture, cypress symbolizes longevity and immortality. In ritual magic, its branches are widely used to channel the energies of the "beyond," and its leaves are burned to provide "ascension" to those who have gone from this world but have not yet found rest. Use it to consecrate charm bags to develop clairvoyance or to promote contact with other planes of existence.

- **Estragon oil** (Artemisia dracunculus)—Venus Oil: This oil, extremely popular in modern esoteric shops and homeopathy stores, is extracted from the plant of the same name to treat arthritis-related pains. It is normally combined with rose oil and orchids to create the popular "oil of Venus," which is essential in multiple rituals and love spells.

- **Eucalyptus**: Eucalyptus essential oil has a unique, fresh, and highly decongestant fragrance, and is used in homeopathic treatments to improve the entry of oxygen to the lungs, reduce bronchial inflammation, and treat the respiratory tract. Eucalyptus essential oil is a natural anti-viral, anti-bacterial, antiseptic, and anti-inflammatory. It is commonly used to treat infectious diseases, bronchitis, and flu and to reduce fever. It has strong healing properties and is an ally of the immune system. Use it to consecrate charm bags for all kinds of healing. Add eucalyptus leaves and rosemary to a bag of green cloth and wear it around your neck when you feel congested or physically weak. This helps speed recovery and prevents a worsening of your condition.

- *Fennel*: The essential oil extracted from sweet fennel—not to be confused with the oil extracted from bitter fennel—is used in stimulating therapies to open the chakras and balance the aura. It helps you be more cautious and practical and makes the most of your talents. According to oral tradition, the essential oil obtained from the seeds of fennel acts as an astral guard against all kinds of bad influences. Draw a magic circle of protection under your bed using this oil to prevent any kind of mental or astral attacks at night while you are asleep.

- *Frankincense*: Essential oil of frankincense, or olibanum, comes from an aromatic resin commonly used to create incense for religious purposes. The essential oil is used in homeopathy as an anti-depressant. It is highly balsamic and tranquilizing and is used as a natural sedative and relaxant. It also gives inner strength and increases the spiritual presence of an individual. Use it to bless and consecrate charm bags intended to provide spiritual strength or connect with higher planes.

- *Geranium*: The essential oil of geranium—specifically that of rose geranium—is widely used in perfumery and naturist cosmetology for making delicate perfumes of long duration. It moisturizes and treats problems with oily skin and promotes regeneration of battered flesh. This highly aromatic oil is a completely natural astringent strong enough for all kinds of skin problems. It is also frequently used as an antiseptic, an analgesic, and as an anti-degenerative in alternative medicine. It is used in certain rituals of white magic and naturist Wicca to treat depression linked to past situations or lack of self-esteem. Use a few drops of it to bless gems and dried herbs that are part of charm bags for protection or to fill your life with blessings.

- *Ginger*: The essential oil of ginger is used in homeopathic medicine mostly as an alternative to chemical pharmaceuticals. This oil is very useful and complex, and is often used as a natural antiseptic, a bacteriocide, an expectorant, and a stimulant analgesic. It is also used in Traditional Chinese Medicine to treat diseases related to "moisture," like rheumatism and catarrh, as well as to strengthen the immune system. In modern witchcraft, it is used to treat very low mood, self-esteem issues, and pessimism, as well as in magical rituals that motivate you to persevere or help you find a guide and right direction. Use it to consecrate charm bags to stimulate confidence, perseverance, proactiveness, and willpower.

- *Immortelle*: The essential oil of immortelle is recognized in homeopathic medicine and naturopathic cosmetics as an excellent cell regenerator for the skin. It is used as an anti-aging treatment and as an anesthetic, an anti-bacterial, an anti-coagulant, an anti-inflammatory, and an anti-viral. In certain alternative treatments, it is also used to provide relaxation and to fight stress, nervousness, sadness, and insomnia. In white magic, it is used to consecrate the cradles of newborns and wish them a long and prosperous life. It is also used to bless magical tools that bring good luck. Use it to consecrate charm bags to attract prosperity and protection, and any amulets you make to protect someone else.

- *Iris*: The essential oil extracted from the roots of the Florentine and German iris is widely used as a strong expectorant, an anti-inflammatory, and a diuretic. In homeopathic medicine, it is used to treat bronchitis, asthma, and some gastrointestinal conditions. The exotic fragrance of this oil makes it suitable for consecrating and blessing all sorts of talismans and charm bags linked to love, physical attraction, sensuality, and passion. Use a few drops of it to recharge an old love charm on a Friday night.

- *Jasmine*: The essential oil of floral jasmine is renowned for its delicious fragrance and mediumistic qualities associated with clairvoyance and precognition. In aromatherapy, it is used as a powerful aphrodisiac and muscle relaxant. In homeopathy and naturopathic medicine, it is known as an analgesic, an anti-depressant, an antiseptic, and a healing anti-inflammatory. It is a good oil to keep on hand to complete a natural emergency kit. It is also frequently used in perfumery, and is widely used as an incense or fragrance for meditation, in relaxation therapies, or even to promote sleep. In white magic and sorcery, it is used to treat minor wounds and skin infections. Use a few drops to scent charm bags intended for relaxation and peace of mind, or to induce prophetic dreams.

- *Juniper*: The essential oil distilled from juniper berries is commonly used in South American homeopathic medicine to treat and/or delay diabetes. It is also used by midwives to accelerate delivery and reduce ailments related to childbirth. The oil is antiseptic, diuretic, sedative, and anti-depressant, and is commonly used in holistic treatments to prevent scarring, regain lost youth, and cleanse oily skin. Use it to anoint charm bags intended to dispel the pain of childbirth and regain lost vitality.

- **Kalanit Oil** (Poppy anemone)—Aphrodite Oil: The oil extracted from the colorful anemone flowers is usually obtained at a very high price on the market, especially as it is the national flower of Israel. These flowers are dedicated to Aphrodite, Greek goddess of love and beauty, and this plant is often linked to the myth of the birth and death of Narcissus. Its essential oil (sold in the market as oil Aphrodite) has a subtle aroma, which according to folklore "awakens the deepest passions," stimulates us to love and lets us love, is used to attract love and convince people to reach marriage. It is perfect to consecrate any object that will be given to a couple.

- **Laurel**: This essential oil is commonly used in white magic to bring good luck, creative inspiration, and friendship. Use a few drops of it to anoint your personal belongings and photographs. It can also be used to consecrate charm bags intended to attract good fortune and promote social relations.

- **Lavender**: Essential oil of lavender is a popular fragrance in much of the world. Its refreshing and stimulating scent promotes relaxation and inner calm. It also has the power to harmonize homes and provide mental clarity. It is used in homeopathic medicine for its many properties, as well as in the manufacture of Bach flower remedies for people suffering from some form of depression or persistent melancholy. The cosmetics industry adds it to a wide variety of creams and perfumes. It is analgesic, antiseptic, anti-inflammatory, and sedative in nature. In white magic, both the flowers and the oil are used to make infusions for beauty and healing talismans, or to take care of children. Use it to consecrate charm bags intended for healing and purification.

- **Lemon**: Lemon essential oil is popular for its exquisite and unique fragrance. It is naturally stimulating and energizing, and is considered a strong anti-depressant. It also has many other uses in cosmetology and modern alternative medicine. It is used to combat flu and as an antiseptic, a bacteriocide, and a completely natural insecticide. It prevents scarring and is used to relieve nasal congestion, improve blood circulation, whiten skin spots, and soften all skin types. Like the blossoms, the oil is used to dispel evil thoughts, ward off enemies, and prevent betrayal. Use it to consecrate charm bags for protection and defense against all kinds of negative energies.

- *Marjoram*: This less-known essential oil is used to treat sprains, cramps, and other muscle ailments anywhere in the body. It is a good aphrodisiac and also is analgesic, anti-oxidant, antiseptic, and anti-viral. It is used in different forms of herbal witchcraft, alternative medicine, and homeopathic medicine to treat insomnia, migraines, stress, and anxiety. The essential oil extracted from the flowers and leaves of marjoram was used in ancient Greece as a relaxant to calm nerves and anxiety. In Europe, it was commonly added to bath water. In some forms of sorcery and magic, it was used to anoint the images of deities and spirits who, for some reason, were upset or angered by a mage's actions. This purportedly made them calm and tranquil. Use this oil to bless charm bags designed to nullify attacks of stress and anxiety.

- *Melissa*: Melissa was essential to all practitioners of traditional alchemy. Its flowers were one of the main ingredients of a tonic that claimed to restore youth and attract longevity. The essential oil extracted by distilling the leaves of melissa is a natural, soothing antiseptic and anti-viral. It is used in aromatherapy to help dispel sadness, feelings of inferiority, and anxiety and to combat panic attacks. Add a few drops to a charm bag during its consecration to evoke positive attitudes and regain lost energy and vitality.

- **Mint**: Mint essential oil is a refreshing aromatic oil and analgesic widely used to relieve pain and irritation of the skin and to treat burns. It has even been used as a homemade natural toothpaste. In homeopathy, it is used to reduce fever, stimulate the nervous system, decrease mental fatigue, relieve stings, and increase body sweating. In various currents of spiritualism and Voodoo, it is often used to ward off negativity and malicious spirits. In sorcery, dried leaves of mint are burned at the entrances of a house to dispel witchcraft and curses. Add a few drops to charm bags intended to attract prosperity and wealth.

- **Musk**: This aromatic oil is marketed as one of the most potent natural aphrodisiacs. In homeopathy, it is used to replenish lost male vitality. In perfumery, it is used to develop exquisite scents and creams. In magic, it is used to raise self-esteem and joy. Use it to bless and consecrate charm bags dedicated to love and sexual energy. *Note*: This aromatic oil can be derived from a number of sources, including seeds, wood, and various animals (musk ox, muskrat, musk duck, musk shrew, musk monkey). It was originally derived from the musk deer (*Moschus*), but this species is now threatened by habitat loss and hunters. Be responsible and try to use oil derived from other sources.

- **Myrrh**: This essential oil is extracted from the myrrh tree (*Commiphora myrrha*), and is widely known for its use as a gargle to combat sore mouth and in toothpastes. It has been used since antiquity in the manufacture of perfumes, incense, homeopathic ointments, and some medicines for colds and bronchitis because it strengthens the immune and respiratory systems. It is currently used in alternative medicine to treat hoarseness and arthritis and to stimulate menstruation in women. It is also a known antiseptic, anesthetic, and antiparasitic. In white magic, it is used to protect children against the Evil Eye and to break all kinds of spells, hexes, and curses.

It is also used to bless the ground in preparation for rituals and to purify old talismans. Add a few drops to a charm bag during consecration to avoid its losing its power and to stimulate its protection over you.

• **Neem**: This essential oil is extracted from the fruits and seeds of the neem tree (*Azadirachta indica*), also known as margosa or Indian lilac. It is commonly used to produce a remarkable variety of cosmetic products like soaps, creams, and perfumes. Its primary use, however, is in Ayurvedic medicine. According to Indian tradition, neem oil is effective in treating various skin conditions and immune-system problems. It is also a recognized natural insecticide used to control mosquitoes and prevent mosquito-borne diseases. It is used to treat fever, malaria, and tuberculosis, as well as many other medical conditions. In India, the neem tree is a symbol of perseverance and healing. Use this aromatic oil to bless charm bags to strengthen physical and mental health.

• **Neroli**: Essential oil of neroli, also known as oil of orange blossom or azahar, is obtained directly from orange blossoms. It has many medicinal properties. In Traditional Chinese Medicine, it is recognized as a strong antiseptic, a sedative, an anti-spasmodic, a digestive, and an anti-depressant and is used as a natural moisturizing skin-cell regenerator. In alternative medicine, it is used to treat digestive problems and stimulate growth in infants. In homeopathy, neroli oil and its flowers are used to treat nervous-system damage and combat emotional stress, insomnia, anxiety, depression, and sadness. In modern witchcraft, the oil is used as an aphrodisiac known to attract the beloved and to promote a desired pregnancy. In South America, it is used to anoint figures and dolls that channel a desired lover and protect or cure him or her at a distance. Use it to bless and activate charms bags to attract love and to dispel depression, work stress, sadness, or insomnia.

- **Niaouli**: This aromatic oil is distilled from the bark of the tea tree. It has long played a role in naturopathic medicine as an antiseptic, an anti-bacterial, and a natural anti-viral. It is commonly used to treat urinary-tract infections, herpes, and fungal infections. In white magic, it is used to lighten energy and emotional burdens, while in aromatherapy, it is used to get rid of stress and clear the mind. Use it to consecrate charm bags intended to influence your own emotions positively, to strengthen self-esteem, and to promote positive attitudes.

- **Nutmeg**: This essential oil is an organic product commonly used in modern perfumery because of its delicious sweet nutty aroma and its revitalizing qualities for the body. It is derived from the nutmeg tree and is used as a flavoring in cooking because it provides the flavor and aroma of nutmeg without leaving any coarse particles. In homeopathic medicine, it is used to treat rheumatic pains and digestive discomfort and to replenish energy levels in the body. In modern spiritualism, it is used to consecrate tools and knives that come into contact with herbs and plants in various sessions. Use it to consecrate charm bags intended to restore health and raise the energy levels of the body.

- **Patchouli**: This essential oil, extracted from the dried leaves of the plant, is valued around the world for its exotic and unique fragrance. It is widely used in perfumery and has become a part of popular culture. The essential oil provides a powerful environmental flavoring that has a known sedative effect. In traditional medicine in China and Indonesia, it is used as an aphrodisiac, an anti-inflammatory, an antiseptic, and a natural relaxant. In natural beauty treatments, it is used to stimulate hair growth and protect against fungal infections of the skin, as well as to treat male impotence and prevent circulatory problems. In white magic, it is used to combat mental fatigue and is also believed to prevent hypnosis and involuntary mental interventions and to protect against being dominated by someone else through sorcery. This oil focuses spiritual consciousness, creating a positive body-mind-spirit connection. Use it to anoint and strengthen charm bags dedicated to mental protection.

• *Pine*: The oil extracted from the needles and twigs of pine is highly aromatic. It is quite popular in pharmacology and in aromatherapy for its various attributes, as well as for its distinctive fragrance. It is anti-bacterial, antiseptic, disinfectant, and a natural deodorizer. It is commonly used to stimulate and revitalize in massages and as an organic high-level herbicide. In homeopathic medicine, it is often recommended to help maintain a healthy respiratory system, to achieve emotional-spiritual balance, to counteract depression and lack of faith, and to release repressed impulses. In traditional Bach flower therapy, it is used to combat guilt and depression caused by feelings of low self-worth. Use a few drops to consecrate charm bags dedicated to healing emotional and/or spiritual ailments, or to dispel negative spiritual influences and fears.

• *Rose*: This well-known oil is distilled from the petals of both damask roses (rose castillas) and Roses of Provence (May roses). The first is well known for its use in the famous "rose water." Damask rose petals are combined with sugar to prepare the *gulkand,* an Ayurvedic tonic originating in Pakistan and India. Rose of Provence is commonly used in various sweet-smelling oils and perfumes. Rose oil is used in homeopathic medicine to treat respiratory and circulatory disorders, and to stimulate the nervous system and regulate hormonal balance in women. It is also used to reduce depression and stress caused by situations beyond your control. In aromatherapy, it is used as a powerful aphrodisiac and is a well-known antiseptic, a skin regenerator, an anti-inflammatory, and a relaxant. In white magic, it is used in a variety of rituals linked to love, beauty, friendship, and protection. Carrying a red sack full of rose petals promotes tenderness and positivism. Add a few drops of essential oil of roses to charm bags to attract, strengthen, and balance love and romantic relationships.

- **Rosehip**: This oil is best known today as a replacement for chemical treatments to rejuvenate the skin. It is a vegetable oil with high vitamin content that is widely used in beauty treatments and treatments for regaining lost youth. It is a natural tonic for the skin, used to prevent wrinkles and age spots, as well as for daily anti-aging treatments. In sorcery, it is widely used to anoint candles and perform rituals that prolong life and renew youth and beauty. Use it to consecrate charm bags that stimulate beauty, love, and longevity.

- **Rosemary**: This is perhaps one of the most widely used essential oils today, along with sandalwood, musk, and cinnamon. It has a variety of uses ranging from cosmetics to alternative medicine, as well as magical properties. It is analgesic, anti-depressant, healing, and diuretic and is used to treat aging skin, acne, and dandruff and to stimulate hair growth. It is also widely used in homeopathy to treat migraines, bronchitis, mental fatigue, and muscle aches. In white magic and traditional witchcraft, it is used to soothe headaches, and improve memory and concentration. It can be mixed with sandalwood oil to anoint doors and windows for protection. Use it to consecrate charm bags that attract money and good luck, and protect against evil, as well as for those that strengthen mental abilities and have aphrodisiac properties.

- *Sage*: Essential oil of clary sage (*Salvia sclarea*) is commonly used in perfumery to develop various rejuvenating treatments, and in aromatherapy to treat symptoms of insomnia and cramps. Sage and its oil are used to scare away demons and evil spirits and to ward off the effects of black magic and all forms of negative energy. Shamans, healers, and spiritualists around the world use it to bless and consecrate magical books, conjure spirits, and strengthen psychic vision. According to oral tradition, a few drops of this mystical oil on the forehead helps to reveal the future. Applied behind the ear, it strengthens intuition, enabling you to "hear" alternate planes of existence in more detail. Use it to consecrate charm bags that bring vitality, confidence, inspiration, creativity, and vision.

- *Sandalwood*: This oil, extracted from the wood of sandalwood tree, is extremely smooth, with a woody aroma. It is commonly used for relaxation and meditation, as well as to nourish and hydrate the skin. It is widely used in perfumery and aromatherapy to provide a sense of calm and satisfaction and is used in a variety of perfumes and aromatic creams. In white magic, it is used as a natural protectant and to bless tools for ritual use. Certain practices of sorcery and Voodoo use it to perfume totems, divination objects, and tarot cards. Use a few drops to bless charm bags containing powers of healing and protection.

- *Tea tree*: This essential oil, extracted from tea tree leaves, is widely used in herbal medicine for its healing properties. It is antibiotic, anti-bacterial, antiseptic, anti-inflammatory, and healing, and is an immuno-stimulant. It is commonly used to treat a variety of skin problems like acne, pimples, warts, and herpes, and to treat infected wounds. In white magic and traditional witchcraft, it is used to provide protection and health and to stimulate your own energies and strengthen all kinds of rituals. Use it to consecrate charm bags to provide strength and energy to spells for protection and health.

- *Thyme*: Extracted from the plant's leaves, this oil is known for its herbal scent and is commonly used in homeopathic medicine to treat skin problems and a variety of conditions in different areas of the body. It stimulates circulation, is used to fight all kinds of infections, and is a natural antibiotic with great healing powers. It activates the nervous system and is a great ally of the immune system. In white magic and traditional witchcraft, it is applied on the back of a pillow to ward off nightmares. Use it to consecrate charm bags for protection to significantly prolong their effectiveness.

- *Tuberose*: According to Catholic tradition, this essential oil was used by Mary Magdalene (or Mary of Bethany) to wash the feet of Jesus of Nazareth. In Ayurvedic medicine, it is considered to "influence the body, mind, and spirit at the same time." In aromatherapy and alternative medicine, it is used to stimulate blood circulation and treat skin allergies. It also strengthens the nervous system, fights a variety of phobias, decreases emotional instability, and increases sexual energy. Use a few drops of it to strengthen all kinds of charm bags that influence positive or negative feelings.

- *Vanilla*: This essential oil is often used for perfuming clothes and rooms because of its subtle and romantic fragrance. This sweet floral scent is widely used for perfuming consecrated candles to attract love and joy, and to ward off envy and sorrow. It is anti-depressant, anti-inflammatory, and sedative, and is widely used in aromatherapy for its soothing and aphrodisiac qualities. It also helps fight anxiety and feelings of personal frustration. Anoint a white candle with essential oils of vanilla, sandalwood, and lavender to attract prosperity and joy to the home. In white magic, it is commonly used to enhance psychic energies and implement various forms of magical mentalism—telepathy, empathy, and precognition. Use a few drops to recharge your amulets and magical talismans and to consecrate ritual objects on your altar.

- **Verbena**: This essential oil is a potent sedative, an astringent, an anti-inflammatory, and a digestive commonly used in various alternative medicine treatments. It is used to combat insomnia, nervousness, rheumatism, and chronic diseases and as a folk remedy to relieve headaches and dissipate stress and worries. In Bach flower treatments, it is used to promote wisdom and provide emotional and spiritual strength and to combat religious fanaticism or excessive selfishness. In magic, it is used to protect and heal, to channel angelic essences and virtues, to facilitate new beginnings, and to calm anxiety. Use it to consecrate charm bags that channel higher spiritual entities and to bless new projects.

- **Vetiver**: This essential oil is very popular in perfumery and in Ayurvedic medicine. It is widely used for medical, culinary, therapeutic, energetic, and spiritual purposes. It is also used to repel insects, to treat skin infections, and to resist heart failure. In homeopathy and alternative medicine, it is used to regenerate and firm the skin and to combat various symptoms associated with blood circulation and lymphatic disorders. In white magic, it is used to channel the healing energies of the Earth, dispel spiritual obstacles, and strengthen healing rituals linked to Nature and its spirits. Use a few drops to consecrate charm bags to strengthen any emotional or spiritual aspect and to bless talismans linked to Mother Nature.

- *Yarrow*: Extracted from the flowers and leaves of the plant, this oil is normally used to promote inner peace and calm and to dispel sadness, melancholia, and fear. It removes emotional or creative blocks that can become obstacles in your day-to-day life. In white magic, it is commonly used to strengthen intuition, spontaneity, and eloquence and to harmonize and balance your relationship with the cosmic energies that influence your environment. Yarrow essential oil is a good choice for perfuming talismans and charm bags that balance different aspects of your life or that can somehow help balance your time.

- *Ylang ylang*: This essential oil, distilled from the flowers of the plant, is highly valued in aromatherapy. It relieves hypertension, sedates the nervous system, and relaxes muscles. It also stimulates and strengthens the scalp and increases joy and creativity. In homeopathic medicine, it is a well-known aphrodisiac and is also used to treat problems of negativity, tension in relationships, panic attacks, and lack of creative development. It is a strong anti-depressant that reduces anxiety and also acts as a natural sedative. In white magic, it is used to find employment or get a promotion. Mix it with rosemary and mint oil and rub it on your wallet to attract money and good fortune. Apply a few drops to bless talismans and charm bags tied to money, employment, and wealth.

Chapter 11

Using Animals and Bones in Charm Bags

In African tradition, in modern revivals of the Maori tradition in New Zealand, and in certain forms of traditional witchcraft, charm bags that combine herbs, stones, earth from different places, and the bones of various animals are common. The bones used in these bags often belong to animals or creatures specifically consecrated to the divinities of a particular pantheon. In Africa, and more specifically in Nigeria and Ghana, this is a fairly common practice of the Yoruba tradition. Young practitioners of this tradition hang charm bags made of skin around their necks that contain painted stones of different colors (white, blue, yellow, and red), pieces of metal, and carved bones from several local animals that have been offered in ritual sacrifice to their corresponding deities.

In New Orleans, you can find shops that sell leather pouches filled with aromatic herbs, earth from a local cemetery, and bird bones to bring good luck, love, and fortune. In fact, according to local folklore, Voodoo queen Marie Laveau carried a charm bag that contained several precious stones and gems that matched the carved bones of animals that conferred certain clairvoyant powers and control over Nature. Likewise, most shamanic traditions use bones to complement the magic of a charm bag. These bones, tradition dictates, must be taken directly from the animal as it dies to prevent them from being "disturbed" by external energies. Thus buying bones in local specialty shops is not recommended, although many seem to use this option.

The use of bones in charm bags augments energies that bind you to the forces of Nature. These charm bags are usually made of leather instead of cloth—leather taken from the same animal whose bones are used in the bag. This keeps the spirit of the animal closely bound to the invocation and makes it a "companion," or part of a "family," charged with the protection of the shaman and his family. Those openly dedicated to the practice of shamanism who prefer to reduce the suffering of animals avoid this practice and rather, transfer the essence of their family spirit to their children and future generations through a private ritual in which they deliver a talisman or totem to the young initiate so that, from that moment, the he or she carries the protective spirit of the family.

The bones used in these charm bags are usually taken from the front legs of a coyote, deer, goat, or fox. They are carved by hand with channeling symbols to keep the spirit near the talisman. In some countries, you can buy carved bones from animals like bear, deer, and birds. This is not recommended, however, because it endangers certain species and promotes indiscriminate trafficking in animal bones.

More modern practices, like Wicca and some schools of naturopathic sorcery, prefer to avoid the use of animals entirely in their practices for various reasons, and discourage animal sacrifice, although most experienced practitioners seem to agree that the use of bones from animals that are found dead from other causes—accident or disease—are not appropriate for use in their rites.

The use of bones, feathers, and other animal parts in the crafting and consecration of charm bags depends entirely on the maker. There are many ways to use many different parts from many different animals, and the charm bags that contain them may have many different uses. For example, real feathers of some birds are commonly used in sorcery to carry out forms of magic linked to communication, speed, and acceleration of personal matters, or to conjure the elemental spirits of Air. On the other hand, real feathers are often added to charm bags to strengthen communication, spontaneity, and eloquence, as well as to find a quick resolution to personal problems that have gotten out of control.

In traditional witchcraft, sundried and powdered organs of various animals are often used to stimulate skill and physical endurance, and to accelerate physical recovery or a rejuvenating process. South American folklore tells of a woman who could not have children. She found a dead white dove in front of her home and took it to the village witch, thinking it might be a bad omen. The witch extracted the heart of the bird from its chest with her bare hand, dried it in the sun, and ground it with various herbs. The next day, she handed the woman a skin bag no bigger than the palm of her hand that contained the powder and told her to place it under her bed. Eight months later, the woman gave birth to a healthy baby with a strange five-pointed mark on his chest just to the side of his heart.

According to European tradition, hanging the tooth of a tiger or crocodile as a medal near the heart strengthens virility and sexual potency in a man, while in certain modern European countries, red charm bags containing an alligator tooth and some dried herbs like cinnamon and rosemary are manufactured and sold in esoteric shops for the same purpose.

In Brazil and Venezuela, very small triangular bags of skin containing bones, teeth, graveyard dirt, and aromatic dried flowers are completely sealed and used to promote health and conjure good luck. In Venezuela, as in Colombia, spiritualist traditions share the practice of crafting *contras*—pouches made from the skin of a lamb or goat and filled with seven small bones carved from seven different animals, some herbs with healing or protective qualities, soil collected from seven different places, and a piece of jet. This bag, which is full of secret symbolism, is then consecrated at midnight and "charged" on behalf of a familiar spirit to protect against evil, envy, betrayal, malicious spirits, and witchcraft.

One practice of modern witchcraft involves elements of the European tradition, angelology, and the mystical Kabbalah. It consists of filling a white silk bag the size of a fist with seventy-two real feathers and nine quartz crystals of different colors. These symbolize the seventy-two angels and the nine choirs of the Kabbalah. This amulet is tied with a white-and-gold ribbon with seven knots in it and hung on the front door of a house so that the spirits' caregivers are always welcome. It also attracts happiness and good health, and, at the same time, keeps misfortune from the home.

In certain parts of the Caribbean, it is customary to present a bag of green cloth with seven silver coins and dolphin-shaped carved bones in it to attract wealth and guard against getting lost at sea. In black magic and other perhaps less conventional forms of sorcery, it is customary to consecrate a bag packed with raven and owl feathers—as symbols of clairvoyance and the night—to acquire greater contact with the spiritual plane and to strengthen clairvoyance. According to this tradition, the bag facilitates movement at night with the help of the ravens, using the sight of the owls.

PART III

Charm Bags for Everyday Magic

If you visit the forest, take along a gris-gris bag, like the ones carried by travelers from Sahel. A tiny cloth bag filled with bones, flowers, and herbs protects them from snakes, theft, and bad luck.

Chapter 12

Charm Bags for Abundance and Success

In this chapter, you will learn how to make and consecrate charm bags designed to attract money and to channel the mystical energy of prosperity. That energy can bring job promotions, ensure success in your projects, and encourage recognition by your colleagues and admiration by your superiors. These charm bags are inspired by evolutionary economics and modern marketing practices. They are suitable for merchants and retailers, as well as for independent businesses and entrepreneurs.

In certain cities in Europe, as in much of Latin America, rituals and talismans to fulfill wishes often borrow various elements from Egyptian folklore and gypsy traditions. The following short magical ritual is one such practice that creates what is called a "bag of wishes." This ritual and the charm it creates is packed with symbolism, tradition, and folklore from different cultures. The resulting "all-purpose" magic pouch is a minimalist and much simpler version of charm bags that focus directly on specific desires. If you want to, you can combine this ritual with any of the charm bags given below that are targeted on specific goals. By doing so, you can increase the power of your charm bags, complement your practice, and give yourself a more varied repertoire.

Unless otherwise specified, all charm bags given here need to be consecrated using either the long or short rituals given in chapter 6.

Bag of Wishes

Begin by writing a specific wish on a piece of parchment no bigger than the palm of your hand. Write the wish seven times with magic ink made by mixing ink, ashes, powdered holy cascara, and two drops of your own blood. Roll up the parchment and tie it with a ribbon—preferably red or purple. Place the rolled parchment in a bag of dark leather or purple fabric. This color symbolizes the transformation of your requests from desires to reality.

This traditional bag of wishes works in ways similar to a charm bag and, in fact, is just a different version of those magic pouches. You can increase the power of the pouch by adding herbs and spices—for instance, rosemary, sage, star anise, verbena, or clove—a white quartz crystal, a stick of cinnamon, and a lock of our own hair or some of your own nail clippings. To complete the bag of wishes, add a few drops of aromatic essential oil and consecrate it at night using a white or purple candle to activate its magic.

Charm Bag for Money

Write your entire name on a piece of parchment next to the symbol for the currency used in your country ($ / € / ¥). Write your name and the symbol seven times, using blue or green magic ink, then roll up the parchment and tie it with a green or blue ribbon and place it in a cloth bag that is the same color as the ribbon. You can further strengthen the powers of this charm bag by adding some bay leaves, cloves, rosemary, or mint, and a small piece of quartz. Consecrate it in the light of a green candle. It helps to first cleanse and then charge the ritual area you are working in with sandalwood incense.

To further personalize this charm bag, you can place your own hair or nail clippings and a photograph of yourself in it before consecrating it. If you are making the charm bag for someone else, use his or her hair, nail clippings, and photograph in place of your own.

Charm Bag to Protect Businesses and Increase Sales

On a Wednesday or Saturday night, preferably under a Crescent Moon, fill a bag of green cloth with seven silver coins (these can be coins from different countries), a piece of lemon peel, and a tablespoon of sunflower seeds. Perfume the bag with essential oil of myrrh and ylang ylang.

Charm Bag to Project Your Desires

Fill a bag of gold cloth with dry shredded basil and cascara sagrada root. Add three golden bells, a sunflower, clover, and three silver coins. Consecrate this charm bag during the morning hours on a Sunday using a few drops of essential oil of sunflower or chamomile and a gold-colored candle. Dedicate it in the name of the solar deity of your personal pantheon.

Charm Bag to Achieve Your Goals

Take a piece of brown leather or fabric and fashion a small pouch from it no bigger than your hand. In it, place a piece of garnet, a jet, a jasper, chamomile flowers, dried St. John's wort, and a small bow made with black ribbon. Sew up the bag, closing it completely, then pass it through the smoke of sandalwood incense. Suspend the bag from a black or brown cord and hang it on the doorframe of your bedroom. It will keep you focused on your goals and keep all distractions from interfering with your success.

Charm Bag to Improve Relationships

On the night of the Full Moon in February, make a light-blue cloth bag no bigger than your hand. Fill it with sunflower and papaver seeds, a piece of coral, petals of white chrysanthemum, a small recent photograph of yourself, and a short strand of your own hair. Sew up the bag, sealing it completely, and anoint it with a few drops of essential oil of tangerine and cinnamon. Suspend the bag from a blue cord and wear it around your neck or hang it from the rear-view mirror of your car to enhance friendships and guard against gossip.

Charm Bag to Grant Your Wishes

Fashion a charm bag from azure cloth. In it, place seven corn kernels, seven poppy seeds, seven coffee grains, seven almonds, seven drops of sandalwood oil, a tablespoon of powdered cinnamon, a recent photo of yourself, and seven apple seeds. Place the charm bag on your altar. Every Monday night, light a blue candle and a stick of lily or nutmeg incense next to the bag to give it power.

Charm Bag for Abundance

On the night of the Full Moon in March, make a red cloth bag and fill it with the seeds of seven types of flowers. You can either gather these yourself or buy them. Add white rice, a pinch of cinnamon, and seven silver coins. Perfume the bag inside and out with a few drops of sandalwood oil for good fortune. Suspend the bag from a red ribbon and hang it near your kitchen or pantry so you never have a food shortage in your house.

Charm Bag for Success

Craft a blue or green cloth bag and fill it with rue, rosemary, a pinch of sea salt, ten grains of coffee, ten grains of wheat, one teaspoon of dried mint, and a small magnet.

Charm Bag for Fame and Success

On a Sunday, fashion a bag from gold cloth. Inside it, place a small piece of gold or a gold-plated object. Add a piece of amber, a lock of your own hair, dried lily flowers, and nine drops of essential oil of cedar or roses.

Charm Bag to Balance Feng Shui

On a Monday, craft a red charm bag and fill it with eight Chinese coins (easy to get in specialty shops), three feathers of different colors, pieces of agate and aquamarine, and a pinch of yarrow (Roman chamomile). This talisman will activate positive energies and attract health, abundance, success, and good luck. You can perfume it with your favorite essential oil. Once consecrated, hang it next to the front door of your home or office.

Charm Bag for the Good Fortune of August

A few days before the August Full Moon, prepare an infusion of jasmine flowers, basil, and apple seeds. Craft a green—preferably emerald green—cloth bag the size of your hand and wash it with the infusion three nights in a row, leaving it to dry overnight and washing it again each morning. On the evening before the August Full Moon, anoint a green candle with lavender and jasmine oil. Light the candle next to a stick of lavender incense. Fill the charm bag with basil, apple seeds, ground cinnamon, sandalwood powder, cumin, and cedar leaves. Close it completely and hang it on a green ribbon or cord in a corner of your house so that good fortune and abundance will always smile on you.

Charm Bag to Eliminate Financial Difficulties

The Full Moon of December is the last Full Moon of the year, so it is an important time to craft charm bags that can help you begin the new year without being encumbered by old debts and economic problems. Fill a navy blue or indigo cloth bag with three poinsettias (*Euphorbia pulcherrima*) that have been dried in the sun. Add three crystals of different colors, a high-denomination bill in good condition, a recent photograph of yourself, and three almonds. Seal the bag and perfume it with scents of hyacinth, jasmine, and geranium, or a few drops of your personal perfume. Hide the bag in a corner of your house.

Charm Bag to Resolve Legal Issues
Craft a blue charm bag on a Thursday and fill it with five copper coins, cedar leaves, and a few drops of essential oil of roses.

Charm Bag to Attract Money
Craft a green charm bag and fill it with a teaspoon each of rice, poppy seeds, sesame seeds, cinnamon, sugar, and corn kernels.

Charm Bag for Money, Success, and Good Fortune
Make a pouch out of dark green cloth and fill it with three tablespoons of oak moss, two teaspoons of cedar shavings, one teaspoon of ginger, and a few drops of essential oil of vetiver.

Charm Bag to Recover an Investment
In an olive-green cloth bag, place the bud of a yellow or white carnation, a few drops of peppermint essential oil, a tablespoon of coriander powder, and a tablespoon of fennel powder.

Charm Bag to Strengthen a Business
Make a charm bag from brown or yellow cloth. In it, place a pinch of sugar, some bread crumbs, five pennies, a teaspoon each of grains of benzoin, chopped basil, juniper seeds, and fresh rosemary, and nine drops of peppermint essential oil.

Charm Bag to Improve the Economy

Craft a brown or green cloth bag and fill it with two teaspoons of laurel, one teaspoon of basil leaves, one teaspoon of parsley seeds, and a few drops of peppermint essential oil.

Charm Bag to Attract Happiness and Wealth

In a blue or red cloth bag, place a tablespoon of juniper berries, a teaspoon of ash berries, a teaspoon of holly berries, a teaspoon of almonds, and a teaspoon of ground cinnamon.

Charm Bags for Luck

Here are some charm bags that channel and attract good luck in all aspects of your life.

Charm Bag of Seven Herbs

This charm bag will channel good fortune and make sure that it is present in each and every aspect of your life. On the night of the Crescent Moon, prepare a blue cloth bag and place it on your altar. Anoint the bag inside and out with essential oil of lavender and ylang ylang. Fill the bag with equal parts of angelica, sage, jasmine, lavender, lily, sunflower, and verbena. Consecrate the charm bag and place it on your altar every night to activate good luck.

Charm Bag for Good Luck

In a green or yellow cloth bag, place a teaspoon each of poppy, star anise, nutmeg, and orange flowers. Consecrate the bag on your altar on a date you consider propitious.

Charm Bag to Ward Off Bad Luck

Craft a violet cloth bag. In it, place a teaspoon of parsley, a teaspoon of rosemary powder, a white feather, and nine heads of garlic.

Charm Bag to Turn Bad Luck into Good Luck

Make a purple cloth bag and, in it, place a small amethyst, a white quartz, twelve drops of eucalyptus oil, twelve drops of pine oil, a sprig of oak, and a four-leaf clover.

Charm Bag for Gamblers

Fill a red cloth bag with herb couscous, dried root of laurel, root of the tobacco plant (sometimes referred to as "smoke of the land" in some places), snake root, and mandrake root. Anoint the bag with a few drops of essential oil of lavender and jasmine. After consecrating this bag on your altar, the person who carries it will have better luck when gambling.

Chapter 13

Charm Bags for Physical Health and Balance

Charm bags have many uses—and not only in magic and sorcery. They are also an important tool that connects you with the spiritual world and with Nature. These connections are what allow you to use them for therapeutic purposes and to support holistic processes that can heal you physically, mentally, emotionally, and spiritually.

The human body is a perfect and complex machine adapted to store within it the soul—a spiritual component of essential energy that links us to the universe and to the divine. Your soul is, in fact, the most valuable part of you. It is the spirit and essence that connects you to the universe and to other living beings that inhabit the cosmos. The soul works with the body as part of the evolutionary process, making a perfect package—a vehicle that allows you to draw on knowledge and enduring wisdom during your maturation process, and to interact with other souls. This process can last for years or even decades, until the body, for a variety of reasons, stops working and frees the soul from its bondage. The soul then searches for a new container to inhabit on this or other planes, continuing the evolutionary quest for perfection.

Just as your physical body gets sick and suffers during the process of physical evolution and growth, your soul can also become unbalanced or "infected" by external agents like negative emotions, energetic imbalances, and sudden astral changes caused by diverse factors that can range from a spell cast by someone else to an imbalance in your own karma—which can be much more serious. According to modern metaphysics, as well as traditional belief systems like Kabbalah and Vedic astrology, the negative conditions that affect the spirit can unbalance you completely, causing terrible mood swings, prolonged depression, lack of energy, bad feelings that seem to have no explanation, physical stress, and prolonged sleep disturbances. These conditions can seriously endanger your physical health and lead to instability in your immune system, allowing even the most common illnesses to become serious threats. Both modern metaphysics and Indian medicine agree that holistic therapies that integrate treatment of the body, the soul, the aura, and the chakras can be effective in these situations. We'll talk more about the chakras later in this chapter.

In this chapter, we will look at a number of charm bags that can channel the healing energy of the Earth to treat physical ailments and restore balance to the physical body. You can use these charm bags to carry out healings and cures of all kinds. They are quite organic, simple, and unsophisticated, and do not require complicated preparation or consecration. Do not hesitate to use them to accelerate healing processes or to give yourself some extra support during medical treatment.

Remember, these charm bags can support and accelerate the healing process and even sometimes help prevent disease. But you must not use them to replace proper medical attention or preventive treatment. They just make medical treatment more effective and strengthen your body to fight diseases through their healing energies.

Charm Bag for Health

On a piece of parchment, with magic ink—preferably green—write your full name or the full name of the person you want to heal. After writing the name seven times, roll up the parchment and tie it with a white or green cloth ribbon, then place it in a small bag of the same color. You can further strengthen the power of this charm bag by adding some dried coriander, honeysuckle, sage, or thyme, and a translucent quartz. Consecrate the bag in the light of a green or white candle. If you want to, you can also cleanse and charge the atmosphere before performing the ritual by burning some sage or honeysuckle incense.

Charm Bag for Pest-Related Diseases

This bag can guard against pest-related ailments and insect bites. On the night of the Full Moon in May, craft a small green cloth bag no bigger than your fist. In it, place dirt from a nearby park, jasmine flowers, and equal parts of dried root of liveforever and white tea. Seal the bag and place it under your bed for nine straight nights. On the tenth night, burn the bag on a piece of coal or in a pot.

Charm Bag for Health and Longevity

Craft a white cloth bag. In it, put a piece of agate, a pinch of dried root of dragon's blood, and a teaspoon of white tea.

Charm Bag to Improve Health

If you feel you have had better days, make this simple charm bag and your health will improve. Craft a red cloth bag and fill it with a sprig of St. John's wort, a sprig of St. Lorenzo herb, and a sprig of vulneraria. Scent the bag with essential oil of myrrh and bless it on your altar.

Charm Bag to Accelerate Recovery

On a Wednesday, light a green candle. In its light, craft a white bag and fill it with equal parts of mint, cedar, and ginger. Add a photograph of the person recovering, along with hair, nail clippings, or a piece of jewelry belonging to that person. Consecrate this bag on the same Wednesday night with a few drops of essential oil of anise and basil. Keep it on your altar to charge it for a night or two before delivering it.

Charm Bag to Accelerate Healing

Fashion a pouch from a light-green fabric and fill it with a mixture of a tablespoon each of dried angelica root, saffron, carnation, and gardenia. Add a piece of amethyst, a white quartz, a pinch of dirt or sand from a nearby park, and nail clippings of the sick person. Consecrate the bag on a date you consider propitious for the person and the situation.

Charm Bag to Cure Insomnia

In a light-blue cloth bag, place dried willow root, chamomile. and lime flowers. Add a few drops of essential oil of vetiver and consecrate the bag with a ritual using lavender incense.

Charm Bag to Induce Sleep

Craft a pink charm bag and fill it with a teaspoon of dried chamomile flowers, a teaspoon of dried mint leaves, a tablespoon of ground ginger, and a tablespoon of nutmeg powder. Save this charm bag for use whenever someone in your home has difficulty falling asleep. Just place it under that person's pillow and sleep will come.

Charm Bag to Fight Exhaustion

This charm bag gives you a boost of energy during the day. Craft an orange cloth bag and fill it with equal amounts of roots of elm, gorse, rhododendron, and olive. Add a few drops of your personal perfume. Every time you feel exhausted or lacking in energy, hold this charm bag close to your chest with both hands.

Charm Bag to Fight Anemia

Make a pouch from white cloth and fill it with equal parts of gorse, olive, and rosehip dried and crushed together to make a powder. Give this bag to the person suffering from anemia and, in a few days, it will start to have an effect.

Charm Bag for Fertility I

This charm bag can help those who can't have children or who are having difficulty conceiving. Make a pink cloth bag and fill it with nine petals of pink roses, an amulet or item with the symbol of the planet Venus on it, some cloves, and one beryllium gem. On the night of the Crescent Moon, prick your finger with a sterile needle and anoint the amulet with a few drops of your blood. Then stain an oval-shaped garnet with one drop of your blood and place it in the bag. Light a strawberry-, cinnamon-, or cherry-scented candle and consecrate the charm bag in its light. Every night, place this bag under the bed where you make love.

Charm Bag for Fertility II

Craft a brown cloth bag and fill it with two tablespoons of dried root of honeysuckle, two tablespoons of evergreen, a piece of onyx, a piece of garnet, and a small loop made with pink, violet, and baby-blue ribbon.

Balancing the Aura

The aura is an external projection of the soul. Because of this, you can treat negative conditions of the soul in many different ways through it. The aura is divided into seven layers of light, or seven energy skins, that are aligned with each of the seven chakras in the body (more on the chakras below). Each of these layers of light contains the different colors reflected by different aspects of your cosmological and spiritual awareness.

Your own aura may reflect your various physical or spiritual discomforts, which is why you can carry out a complete healing of your own body through its therapeutic stabilization. To do this, you use various holistic techniques combined in various charm bags that can return you to spiritual equilibrium.

Charm Bag to Balance the Aura

To balance and cleanse your personal aura, use this quick magical ritual. Purify a piece of quartz crystal by immersing it in a glass of water mixed with a tablespoon of salt. Let the crystal sit in the water for at least twenty minutes, then remove it. Light an incense stick of camphor, mint, or sunflower, and a white candle. Pass the purified crystal through the incense smoke several times and then, very carefully, through the flame of the candle. Place the crystal inside a small purple bag and fill the bag with laurel, camphor, and peppermint, and a flower of cotton or a sun-dried white chrysanthemum. Completely close the bag and perform the short consecration ritual given in chapter 6 to enhance its energies.

Once consecrated, hold this charm bag in your right hand (your left, if you are left-handed). With your eyes closed, breathe deeply and slowly three times, then pass the bag all over your body—arms, legs, torso, and especially your chest and neck—allowing it to absorb all external negativity. Hold the bag for a few minutes on the top of your head, exerting a slight pressure to draw in all the inner calm and tranquility you can while the charm bag does its job.

Open your eyes and place the charm bag in a corner of the room. *Do not put it on your altar!* Put a glass of purified water next to the bag and light a white candle. The candle flame will consume any negative energy that was absorbed by the charm bag, while the glass of purified water will prevent any negative energies from escaping. Finally, put the charm bag aside after the candle has burned down completely. Repeat this cleansing operation whenever you feel necessary, or perform it each week to prevent future problems.

Charm Bag to Heal and Strengthen the Aura

If you want to make a charm bag that you can take with you for spiritual healing and protection, use this simple process. Invoking this kind of protection will, in turn, rid your "spiritual skin" of any negative energy and give it more power to prevent spiritual imbalances.

Fill an orange cloth bag with three small pieces of quartz crystal, a tablespoon of rock salt or sea salt, and equal parts of myrrh and wormwood. Consecrate the bag and take it with you everywhere to heal, strengthen, and protect your spiritual expression.

Balancing the Chakras

The Hindu tradition, Tibetan Buddhism, and contemporary Western esoteric practices all recognize the chakras as centers of pure vital energy located throughout our astral bodies and linked by energetic pathways that transmit energy and distribute it according to the body's needs. The chakras stimulate the work of the nervous system and the endocrine glands, which gives them a direct influence on the development and control of different hormones that regulate mood and overall health.

The human body has seven chakras that are aligned astrally along the spinal cord, which keeps them connected, in turn, to the Earth element and the higher astral planes. The chakras thus fulfill an important task as astral organs, as they distribute along the body all the energy we have, which affects our diverse organs and muscles. From time to time, however, these tiny energy machines must be balanced and treated to ensure that they are working perfectly—just as the parts of a car must be checked every so often to avoid potential breakdowns. You can balance your chakras through holistic therapy with charm bags using two different approaches: direct and indirect. Both are effective and achieve the same results, but to understand why, you have to understand how each approach works.

The direct approach to balancing the chakras requires that you prepare a small cloth bag of the representative color for each chakra to be cleared (see chapter 7). Fill the bag with the appropriate gems or stones (see chapter 9), cleansing each one first by putting it for a few minutes in a glass of water mixed with salt. Consecrate the pouch by passing it clockwise through smoke from a stick or cone of incense of myrrh. Then place the charm bag on the site of the chakra you want to clear. The pouch will absorb any negativity there so the chakra can resume its work and regain its proper energetic frequency.

Each of the seven chakras regulates different organs and, therefore, different energies.

- *First chakra (Sahasra-ara)*: located at top of the head and shaped like a lotus flower whose petals never stop growing. This chakra is linked to space, trust, divinity, and ascension; its colors are white and purple. To clear it, make a bag of white or purple cloth and fill it with a piece of amethyst, a piece of diamond or selenite, and a piece of quartz crystal.

- *Second chakra (Ajna)*: located on the third eye between the eyebrows. It regulates the pineal gland and is shaped like a lotus with two petals. This chakra is associated with intuition, prevention of danger, courage, clairvoyance, and all forms of extrasensory perception. Its colors are indigo and violet. To clear it, craft a cloth bag of violet or dark-blue cloth and fill it with a piece of quartz crystal and a piece of amethyst, moonstone, lapis lazuli, or sodalite.

- *Third chakra (Vishuddha)*: located in the throat and shaped like a lotus with sixteen blue or turquoise petals. This chakra is associated with the ether, the sense of taste, communication, mastery of language, and self-expression. Its color is blue. To clear it, fill a blue cloth bag with a piece of quartz crystal and a piece of aquamarine, turquoise, or lapis lazuli.

- *Fourth chakra (Anahata)*: located in the heart and shaped like a lotus with twelve green petals. It is usually represented by a six-pointed star that symbolizes the union of male and female aspects. This chakra is associated with Air, love, compassion, devotion, healing, and the immune system. Its color is green. To clear it, make a green cloth bag and fill it with a piece of quartz crystal or a piece of green or rose quartz, and a piece of jade, emerald, green tourmaline, or green calcite.

- *Fifth chakra (Manipura)*: located in the solar plexus and has the shape of a yellow lotus with ten petals. This chakra is linked to Fire and the Sun and influences the personality, character, energy, freedom, sexuality, and willpower. Its color is yellow. To clear it, use a yellow cloth bag filled with a piece of amber and a piece of agate, yellow topaz, citrine quartz, or tiger's eye.

- *Sixth chakra (Svadhisthana)*: located in the sacrum and manifests as a lotus of six orange petals. This chakra is connected to Water and the Moon, and influences sensuality, the reproductive system, emotions, energy, creativity, and the power to carry out any form of magic. Its color is orange. To clear this chakra, make an orange cloth bag and fill it with a piece of amber and a piece of coral, agate, carnelian, orange calcite, or orange citrine.

- *Seventh chakra (Muladhara)*: located just below the perineum and shaped like a lotus with four large red petals.

It is linked to Earth, Nature, and balance, and directly influences the survival instinct, security, and your own ability to adapt
to your environment. It is the base chakra that directs and "distributes the energies of the Earth element and is your point of connection with it. Its color is red. To clear negative influences on this chakra, fill a red or burgundy cloth bag with three red or black stones. They can be ruby, garnet, red jasper, black tourmaline, obsidian, onyx, red coral, hematite, or black tourmaline.

Charm Bag to Balance the Chakras

This charm bag clears the chakras using the indirect approach. In the early hours of the day on a Wednesday, craft a white charm bag and fill it with seven stones of seven different colors corresponding to the seven chakras—purple or white, violet, blue, green, yellow, orange, and red. Purify the stones first in water mixed with salt. Then place them one by one into the charm bag and add a small lock of your own hair to personalize the ritual. Consecrate the bag and meditate for a few minutes holding the charm bag in both hands. Take a few minutes just to meditate. Breathe deeply and slowly, and relax while the charm bag does its job. Repeat this ritual once or twice a month. You will soon notice positive changes in your state of mind, your mood, your self-esteem, and your overall health.

Charm Bag to Energize the Chakras

Craft a violet cloth bag from a strong fabric and fill it with a piece of all the following stones: aquamarine, amethyst, amber, aventurina, azurite, chalcedony, rose quartz, white quartz, blood jasper, lapis lazuli, obsidian, and opal. Bless the bag on your altar using the full consecration ceremony given in chapter 6.

Chapter 14

Charm Bags for Love and Attraction

In this chapter, we'll look at charm bags charged with energies to attract love in every one of its forms. These more traditional charm bags are designed to channel the universal energy of love, connect with the essence of amorous attraction, and promote passion between lovers.

These bags will be particularly potent when made on a Friday in the evening hours. To better channel this energy, I suggest you keep them on your altar or in whatever corner of your home you use for your magical work. A red tablecloth and some red flowers on your altar will help to enhance the power of these spells.

Charm Bag for Love

On a piece of parchment (or white paper), write your full name seven times in red ink. Roll up the parchment and tie it with a ribbon of thin red cloth. Place the rolled parchment in a charm bag of the same color that you have prepared in advance. Add a stick of cinnamon, some dried leaves and flowers of the acacia tree, some basil, clove, and jasmine, a pink quartz, and a heart-shaped quartz crystal or rose quartz. Consecrate the charm bag at night under the light of a pink or red candle. If you want to, you can cleanse and prepare the atmosphere in your ritual area by burning a stick or cone of jasmine, cinnamon, or rose incense.

Charm Bag to Attract the Opposite Sex I

This is an old family recipe for attracting the opposite sex. At noon on a Friday, burn some sage and apple tree leaves on a saucer, then anoint the ashes with a few drops of honey and a little essential oil of Aphrodite, oil of Venus, or cinnamon. Light a red or pink candle (to symbolize femininity) and a blue or indigo candle (to symbolize masculinity) and let them burn down completely. This will channel the universal energies of both poles (male and female). At midnight of the same day, collect the ashes and the melted wax from the two candles, put them together in a mortar, and grind them along with a teaspoon of vanilla. Place this mixture in a small pink or sky-blue cloth bag and consecrate it on your personal altar in the smoke of an incense that you choose for the occasion. Place this charm bag under your bed for three to six nights to further bond with it, then carry it with you to capture the attention of the opposite sex.

Charm Bag to Attract the Opposite Sex II

To craft this charm bag, you must first perform a spell and then channel its power into the bag. While this may sound complicated, it is really extremely simple and very effective.

Find or make two candles—preferably red or, alternatively, white—that are shaped in human form, one male and one female. On the back of both candles, draw the astrological symbol of the planet Venus (the mirror of Venus) and anoint both candles with oil of musk and orange blossom. Tie the candles together, facing each other, with a red ribbon. Consecrate them on your altar and then light them. Let them both burn down completely.

When the candles are extinguished, wrap their remains—ashes and melted wax—in a small piece of red or purple fabric. Tie the cloth closed with a red or white ribbon and anoint the resulting bundle with a little honey. Place the bundle in a sachet of red, white, or purple cloth and add some dried orange flowers or dried lemon peel. Seal the sachet and consecrate it. Hang this sachet around your neck with a red string or ribbon, keeping it close to your heart, to conquer the hearts of the opposite sex.

Charm Bag to Attract the Opposite Sex III

According to the old tradition of shamans and healers of South America, carrying a bag full of cumin and a little anise will help you attract the love of the opposite sex. If you want to create something a little more personalized, fill a red charm bag with a tablespoon of cumin, a tablespoon of star anise, a tablespoon of brown sugar, five bay leaves, and a red flower dried in the sun. Consecrate this magical bag anytime between Wednesday night and dawn on Saturday.

Charm Bag to Attract the Same Sex I

If you want to channel the energy of love and romance, and use it to establish a lasting and prosperous relationship with people of your same gender, here's a charm bag that can help.

On one of the magical nights of the year—Walpurgis night, the night of San Juan, Samhain, or even Valentine's Day night (because of the symbolism of the holiday)—collect three nuts (acorns, or almonds)—from a nearby park, three birch leaves, and three small flowers (preferably dandelions). Place them together on your altar on a piece of red cloth and leave them there for several days. In the early morning hours on a day of your choice—either a Friday or one of those wonderful days when Venus is approaching the Earth—consecrate the items one by one and place them inside a cherry-red charm bag. Add a piece of rose quartz or a tulip bulb, seal the bag, and consecrate it on your altar by invoking your personal pantheon.

Charm Bag to Attract the Same Sex II

Here is a modified version of the charm bag described above. Buy two red candles in a specialty shop or catalog that are shaped in human form, both corresponding to your gender. Consecrate both candles on your altar, anointing them with a mixture of honey and essential oil of rose and musk oil.

Light the candles on your altar and let them burn down completely. Draw the symbol of the planet Venus on a piece of parchment with red ink. On the back of the parchment, draw the symbol of your astrological sign. Anoint the paper with the same mixture you used to anoint the candles and place it in a bag of red cloth. Add the remains of the consumed candles and a symbol or drawing of the Chinese *taijitu*—better known as the yin-yang symbol. Seal the bag and consecrate it on your altar. Carry this powerful talisman hung around your neck near your heart. In the evening, you can hang it next to your bed to continue channeling its energies.

Charm Bag to Attract the Same Sex III

This charm bag comes from the Afro-Caribbean tradition of Santería. On a Monday in the morning, make a bag of yellow cloth and fill it with a piece of sea snail's shell, two cloves of garlic, a piece of cocoa, and seven coffee seeds. You can make this bag more powerful by adding some rosemary or sun-dried orange flowers. Consecrate it in the light of a yellow candle lit at the edge of a river in the afternoon. This charm bag can be customized by adding your own hair, or that of the user if the bag is a gift. It becomes even more powerful if consecrated inside a magic circle made of honey on a river bank.

Charm Bag to Bless a Relationship

Use this charm bag to enshrine a loving relationship and fill it with blessings. First, pick up a piece of seashell from a beach. On a Friday night when the Moon is in the astrological sign of Taurus—or on one of those magical days when the morning star (Venus) is seen closer than usual—place your seashell inside a light-pink cloth pouch. Add a piece of coral, a pink quartz—either heart-shaped or with a heart carved into it—and dried pieces of laurel, benzoin, marjoram, and honeysuckle. Consecrate the bag with a few drops of essential oil of cinnamon or jasmine by passing it through the smoke of a cherry- or strawberry-scented candle lit at midnight. This will channel the Venus energy. Keep the bag in a place near the bed where both members of the relationship sleep.

Charm Bag for Luck, Love, and Success

Craft a pink charm bag and fill it with a small acorn, twelve sunflower seeds, a cinnamon stick, a teaspoon of sweet clove, and a few sprigs of oak. Scent the bag with essential oil of benzoin and patchouli.

Simple Charm Bag for Love

Craft a bag from red cloth and fill it with seven apple seeds, seven pomegranate seeds, seven red rose petals, a piece each of turquoise and aquamarine, a pink quartz (preferably heart-shaped), seven drops of musk oil, and seven drops of essential oil of rose. Consecrate the bag (preferably on a Friday) using the full consecration ritual given in chapter 6.

Charm Bag for Newlyweds

This is a simple charm bag that will grant love and happiness to a friend or family member who just got married. Sew together a white cloth bag—preferably silk—and fill it with dried ginger root, a teaspoon of lavender, copal resin, pine or myrrh resin, a small aquamarine, and a rose quartz. Charge the bag with your best wishes as you add each item. Consecrate the bag and give it as a gift to the lucky couple, with instructions that they should keep it under their bed or somewhere in their bedroom.

Charm Bag to Resolve Jealousy

Sometimes that special someone can get so jealous that your relationship starts to suffer. When this happens, you need to dampen that feeling. Craft a red charm bag and fill it with equal parts of roots and flowers of willow, aspen, and holly, a tablespoon of the plant known as "cat's claw," and a lock of your partner's hair. You can carry this bag with you, keep it in your bedroom, or place it under the bed you share.

Charm Bag to Move On

If you need to pull yourself together after a breakup, this charm bag will help you cope with the struggle and move on. Craft a purple charm bag and fill with five bay leaves, two teaspoons of pine needles, lemon peel, and geranium cuttings.

Chapter 15

Charm Bags for Mental Health and Balance

In this chapter, you'll learn about charm bags that can channel various aspects of daily energy, manage different frequencies, and combine different "multi-energetic" elements. These bags can help you improve various aspects of your life that may require adjustment or change.

Happiness is an individual subjective state. All of us are not made happy by the same things. In fact, happiness is closely linked to your mental state and your emotional stability. So these charm bags focus on stimulating these aspects of your life using magical elements to achieve perfect balance. For them to succeed, you must observe in detail what needs to change in yourself and in your surroundings, then channel the forces and energies that you need in your life.

Charm Bag to Dispel Negative Feelings

If you want to make a charm bag to dispel negative feelings, sadness, depression, and tendencies to vice, fill a black fabric bag with a piece of jet or onyx, a piece of quartz crystal, and a small drawing of the yin-yang symbol. You can also add some dried angelica root, and some thistle and wormwood that has been blessed. Consecrate this bag in the flame of a black candle and hold it against your chest whenever you feel sad or depressed. Keep it with you to prevent depressive attacks. Channel into it all negative feelings, including feelings related to fear and worry. After several weeks, when you feel better, bury the bag in a park, off a patio, or in a garden, burying with it all the negative feelings it has absorbed.

Charm Bag for Happiness
Craft a violet cloth bag and fill it with a piece of aquamarine, a pinch of saffron, a pinch of ground cinnamon, a pinch of clove, and a tablespoon of sesame seeds. Consecrate it on your altar on a propitious date of your choosing, then carry it around with you.

Charm Bag to Combat Negativity
Craft an orange charm bag. In it, place seven pink rose petals, seven drops of rose oil, seven drops of orange oil, seven drops of jasmine oil, and a small rock you picked up yourself from a park or nearby river.

Charm Bag for Harmony
Make a green cloth bag and fill it with a pinch of basil, five elderberry leaves, five cloves, five drops of sandalwood oil, five drops of chamomile oil, five drops of ylang ylang oil, a teaspoon of sea salt, a teaspoon of white pepper, and a few leaves of cedar or willow.

Charm Bag to Fight Depression
Make a yellow cloth bag and fill it with equal parts of the following herbs, previously crushed and reduced to the finest powder possible: wild mustard, aspen, cerasifera, gentian, heath, and crabapple. You can scent this bag with a few drops of ginger and cinnamon oils after you seal it, but before you consecrate it. Carry this bag with

you everywhere until you feel better. Then set it aside until you feel as if you may be falling into depression again.

Charm Bag to Turn Enemies into Friends

On a white candle in human form, write the name of the person who is complicating your life with enmity. Anoint the candle with essential oil of mint and light it. When the candle has burned down completely, place the wax remains next to a photograph of the person. Fill a black cloth bag with a tablespoon of marjoram powder and two tablespoons of ground laurel to absorb the negative thoughts of the person and their bad intentions. Consecrate this talisman, then place it inside another charm bag—this time, purple to transform any negative thoughts or intentions into positive ones—that has previously been perfumed with essential oil of myrrh. Tie this bag closed with a purple ribbon, making seven knots, and place it next to the photograph of the person.

Charm Bag to Channel the Inspiration of the Muses

Fill a violet or blue charm bag with twelve sunflower seeds, twelve different coins, a piece of unakite, and a piece of opal or turquoise. Consecrate the bag during the day on a Sunday, the day governed by the Sun and solar gods like Apollo, patron of the arts and protector of the muses. Anoint the bag with essential oils of laurel and/or lily and place it in your studio or office to bring inspiration whenever you need it. You can also keep a female statue next to the bag—a feminine deity or some symbolic figure of a woman—to represent the muses.

Charm Bag for Self-Esteem

Self-esteem is essential to leading a healthy and balanced life. This simple but effective charm will help you improve your own image of yourself. Craft a bag from red cloth and fill it with two teaspoons of chicory roots, a pinch of red chestnut, a pinch of heather powder, and a pinch of water violet. Sew the bag closed on all four sides and consecrate it in on your altar on the best day for your zodiac sign. Carry this bag around with you, and, in a few days, you will start to feel better.

Charm Bag to Combat Guilt
This charm bag will help reduce the guilt feelings that sometimes paralyze people in their daily lives. Craft a violet bag and place inside it dried root of verbena, a hint of Scotch pine, and a pinch of liverwort. Seal and consecrate the bag and carry it with you.

Improving Mental Balance

These charm bags are designed to balance your life and your feelings using gems, minerals, and various herbs linked to balance and justice. They will help you assess your own mental balance and evaluate your priorities and mental state.

Use these charm bags if you need to balance your work with your leisure time and develop more "quality time" in your life. Make them to hang in your office to help you manage your schedule intelligently, or give them as gifts to friends and colleagues who seem to live in a constant state of imbalance.

Charm Bag to Adapt to New Environments
In a green cloth bag, place a tablespoon of dried root of centaury, a tablespoon of vine powder, and a half teaspoon of walnut powder.

Charm Bag to Reduce Aggression
In a light-blue cloth bag, place a mixture of holly, willow, and agrimonia, all dried and crushed together to make a powder. You can carry this bag around to reduce your own aggressiveness, or

make one as a gift if you know someone who suffers from being too aggressive. You can also place this bag under your bed or hide one in your workplace to improve the emotional state of your coworkers.

Charm Bag to Dispel Boredom

Sew a violet cloth bag and fill it with equal parts of aspen and clematis powder, a piece of quartz, and a piece of coral. Bless the bag on your altar and keep it with you, especially when you are in your workplace. This will help dissipate your boredom and help you cope with the feeling of not wanting to do some tedious task. In turn, it will also boost your creativity.

Charm Bag to Fight Egocentrism

You can make this charm bag for yourself if you feel that your own ego is pushing people away, or you can give it to someone who has an ego problem of his or her own to encourage a better understanding with that person. In a black cloth bag, place a photograph of the person with the ego problem. Add a tablespoon of crushed oats, a tablespoon of altar oak powder, and some dried root of water violet. (The last one is optional.)

Charm Bag to Decrease Cowardice

Make a brown charm bag and fill it with a teaspoon of mimulus powder, a tablespoon of rhododendron root, and a pinch of white chestnut. After properly sealing the bag and consecrating it, carry it with you to boost your self-confidence and courage.

Charm Bag to Attract Happy Dreams

Craft a white or light-blue cloth bag. In it, place eight drops of essential oil of poppy, eight drops of essential oil of violet, rose petals, two tablespoons of dried and ground verbena, and dried lavender flowers.

Charm Bag to Ward Off Nightmares

Craft a bag from white cloth and place inside it two teaspoons of chamomile flowers, two teaspoons of lavender flowers, two teaspoons of mint leaves, two teaspoons of ground dried carnations, a piece of orange peel, six drops of oil of lavender, and a lock of your own hair.

Chapter 16

Charm Bags for Protection and Power

This chapter contains several charms for magical and spiritual protection that can link different purposes and objectives—from protecting against the Evil Eye to dispelling deeply buried emotional obstacles that can harm you. Use these powerful charm bags to take care of yourself and others.

Charm bags related to protection stimulate the development of mediumistic powers, which can, in and of themselves, protect against all eventualities. They also provide an extra boost to the energies of your personal aura—enough to ward off evil thoughts, jealousy, and external grudges that may develop in the workplace.

Charm Bag for Family Protection

On a piece of parchment, write the names of those who constitute your closest group of family and friends. Use magic ink—both blue and green, if possible. Put each person's zodiacal sign next to his or her name, then roll up the parchment and tie it with a white fabric ribbon. Place the rolled-up parchment in a white cloth bag and add some dried and crushed basil, garlic, mint, juniper, or St. John's wort, along with a piece of crystalline quartz. Consecrate the bag overnight in the light of a white candle. If you have a photograph in which all family members and friends appear, you can also add it to the charm bag.

Charm Bag for Protection While Sleeping

On the night of the Full Moon in April, craft a small pouch of orange cloth—preferably felt. Place in it a few sprigs of rosemary, basil, and mint, a natural feather, and a small mirror. Seal the pouch and scent it with drops of geranium or sunflower oil. Hang it from a yellow cord on one side of your bed to protect you while you sleep.

Charm Bag to Clear Negative Energies and Attract Tranquility

On a Thursday, or on the eighth day of the month, craft a white or silver charm bag (or you can use both colors) and fill it with cascarilla (powdered egg shell), two tablespoons of pure or powdered cocoa, eight small white feathers, a pinch of camphor, and four or eight silver coins. Consecrate the bag with cocoa and cocoa essential oil on a Thursday morning and place it in the corner of the house closest to the entrance door. This will absorb negative energies in the home and transmute them into calm, peace, and harmony.

Charm Bag to Remove Obstacles

According to African folklore, a bag of dark color filled with twelve small pieces of metal with different shapes (they can be different metals) removes any obstacle from your path. Make this talisman on a Monday or a Thursday after the Full Moon to make it more powerful. You can also add a sprig of white pepper, a tablespoon of sea salt, and some dried and ground leaves of wormwood. Perfume the bag with a few drops of essential oil of cinnamon, bergamot, or lavender.

Charm Bag for Personal Protection

Craft a green or brown charm bag and fill it with nine bay leaves, nine white or red rose buds, a pinch of flour, and nine drops of peppermint oil.

Charm Bag for Protection While Traveling

In a light-green or white cloth bag, place two tablespoons of dried hyssop, two tablespoons of sugar, two tablespoons of crushed mint leaves, an orange blossom, and a small picture or symbol of the place you are going to visit.

Charm Bag to Protect a Garden

Make a dark-green bag and fill it with leaves of different bushes from your garden, dried root of siempreviva, six drops of patchouli essential oil, an empty chrysalis, and two tablespoons of mustard seeds. Consecrate this bag on your altar in the light of both a green and a violet candle. When they have burned down completely, bury their remains beside the charm bag in the north corner of your garden.

Charm Bag to Protect Against Divination and Psychics

On the night of a Crescent Moon, craft a pouch—preferably dark blue or indigo—and fill it with two parts verbena and one part asafetida. Add a tiny crystal pyramid and some soil from consecrated ground. Rub the amulet on your forehead every morning before leaving home. This charm bag is often used by sorcerers who want to keep a low profile or hide from enemies.

Charm Bag to Ward Off Witches and Ghosts

Create a violet charm bag and, in it, place some myrrh, a few pins and needles, some nails, a tablespoon of black pepper, dried flowers of cayenne, and six petals of white rose. Consecrate it on a Saturday night and bury it near the entrance of a cemetery.

Charm Bag for Favors from Nature Spirits

On the night of the Full Moon in June, buy or make a leather or artificial leather bag and fill it with one piece of blood jasper, small amounts of laurel, jasmine, cedar, oak, and narcissus, and eight mint leaves. Scent the bag with peppermint oil and seal it completely. Hang this bag from a green or brown cord at least two meters long, then bless it on your altar. Tie it to a nearby bush or a tree branch to enjoy the protection of Nature spirits.

Charm Bag to Summon Fairies

If you want to bless your garden or a small green space in your home with the presence of fairies, fill a bag of glossy pale-pink or light-green fabric with three pieces of rose quartz, fresh white flowers from orange, lemon, or citron plants, two cinnamon sticks, some poppy seeds, and two small bells. Consecrate this bag at dawn—preferably on a Monday—with essential oil of water lily or any floral oil of your choice. Keep it in your garden or in a quiet space in your home. You can also hang it from the branches of a floral bush or keep it on an altar dedicated to magic with fairies.

Charm Bag to Weaken Warlocks

Fill a purple or black bag with seven tablespoons of soil from seven different places, two tablespoons of coarse salt, a tablespoon of black pepper, and some dried root of verbena. Add a quartz crystal and one personal item of the warlock or sorcerer in question—a photograph, a lock of hair, nail clippings, or his full name and the symbol of his zodiacal sign written on the back of a lemon or orange peel. Consecrate this talisman on a Tuesday night and bury it in a garden or courtyard near the house of the warlock you want to weaken. Alternatively, you can bury it in a pot of soil on his property.

Charm Bag to Repel Witches

This is a popular old Caribbean spell that I have modified to make more effective and less complicated. On the night of a waning Moon, prepare a powdered mixture of charcoal, pepper, and parsley. Add essential oil of vervein, myrrh, and lemon and mix well. Use this mixture to draw a small pentagram on white paper, then fold the paper four times and bless it on your altar, passing it several times through the smoke of myrrh incense. Place the scented drawing inside a small brown or black cloth bag, then add a small symbol of the Egyptian ankh, some sun-dried lemon seeds, some dried ground white flowers, and a touch of white pepper.

Consecrate this bag between midnight and the first hour of the morning to activate its power, then keep it in a corner of your house or bury it in a nearby garden. According to popular folklore, this old talisman will keep witches with bad intentions away from your home.

Charm Bag to Provide Rest to the Dead

To provide rest to those who have departed this world, but for some reason are still present among us unable to rest, or to calm an angry spirit who cannot or will not rest, fill a bag of dark cloth or skin with fresh mint and eucalyptus leaves, basil, powdered ginger, garlic cloves, and a small five-pointed star—either a talisman in this shape or a drawing of one. Bury the charm bag near the tomb of, or on an altar dedicated to, the deceased person. This will calm the restless spirit and help it accept its new role in the other world, enabling it to find peace and quietly become a part of the cycle of life and death.

Charm Bag to Fight Envy, Betrayal, and the Evil Eye

A few hours before sunset, fill a black charm bag with seven small pieces of jet and equal parts of willow, St. John's wort, sage, and parsley. Consecrate the bag and perfume it with patchouli essential oil.

Charm Bag to Ward Off Envy

Envy is a powerful evil that can do you serious harm, so when you encounter it, you must ward against it. People are often led to envy you if you are very good at your job, at your studies, or even at social relationships in your own neighborhood. Craft a black bag and fill it with a piece of cotton, two teaspoons of dried yarrow, and a small onyx. Seal the bag and consecrate it on your altar. Carry it with you everywhere to be protected at all times.

Charm Bag to Combat Hypocrisy and Lies

Craft a purple bag and fill it with powdered agrimonia, centaury, larch, and walnut, and a small mirror. Add a few drops of cinnamon oil.

Charm Bag to Stimulate and Strengthen Magical Skills

Those just beginning in magic may feel that their spells and rituals are taking a long time to be effective, or that their results are quick but unsatisfying. This is really very common among those just starting out, either because of inexperience or because they do not know how to properly channel the energies. If this is true for you, craft a green or purple charm bag and fill it with a small pentagram or pentalfa, a rutilated quartz, a piece of sugilite, a piece olibino, and a piece of mother of pearl. Add a pinch of sea salt and perfume the bag with five drops of essential oil of frankicense, verbena, or tuberose. Consecrate this talisman and carry it around your neck for seven consecutive days. After that, keep it on your altar. You can also take it with you when you perform any type of magical spell, meditation, or ritual—especially those involving astral projection.

Charm Bag to Bless a Home

In a lilac bag, place a tablespoon of breadcrumbs, six fresh leaves of basil, six leaves of thyme, and a tablespoon of powdered benzoin. After consecration, keep this charm bag in a corner of the home to be blessed, or bury it in the center of the home's garden.

Charm Bag to Protect the Unborn

During pregnancy, women are often exposed to envy, jealousy, the Evil Eye, and all kinds of negative psychic and emotional manifestations. The unborn child can absorb these negative energies and must be protected from them. In Africa, it is common to protect pregnant women by marking the belly with ash and cemetery soil (symbolizing the protection of the ancestors), while in South America, a purple rope with nine knots in it is consecrated and tied around the belly. All these methods are effective, but, if you want to go a little further, you can consecrate a pink charm bag filled with dry rose petals of various colors, a piece each of amethyst, lapis lazuli, and amber, and a touch of cumin. Seal the bag and, if you wish, tie it to the consecrated purple rope described above to strengthen the protection of the baby and the mother.

Chapter 17

Charm Bags for Mental and Pyschic Powers

These charm bags will strengthen your altar and your various magical purposes. Use them to increase your power and ability to carry out your own personal magic. Place them in key places—beside or beneath your altar, beside your bed, or at the front door of your house. You can also carry them with you to Sabbat celebrations or when you join your coven.

These charm bags stimulate the dormant energy within you and help you break free of your own chains. They will raise magical spirits and help you better understand all the esoteric knowledge that can complement your life and work.

Charm Bag to Awaken Inner Power

On an October night, craft a bag from purple fabric or painted leather. Fill the bag with catnip, sage, and cascara. Then place several pieces of coal in a small cauldron and light them. Add some myrrh and camphor. Hold the charm bag in both hands, visualizing the fire, and throw it into the cauldron with your left hand. This ritual will remove any magical or spiritual blockages that are inhibiting your astral and spiritual powers.

Charm Bag to Strengthen Magical Powers I

Craft a purple bag and, in it, place an image or a recent photograph of yourself. Add seven silver coins, a natural white feather, a teaspoon of crushed and ground almond, a sprig of peppermint, a cinnamon stick, some cloves, and a teaspoon of ginger. This amulet is especially effective if made and consecrated on Samhain or during the first Full Moon of the year.

Charm Bag to Strengthen Magical Powers II

Craft a purple fabric pouch and fill it with equal parts of sage, fennel, ginger, jasmine, and rue. Add a piece of quartz crystal, a moonstone, and a small magnet. Consecrate this bag on Walpurgis night or on Samhain—both known as Hallowe'en in different countries. Keep the consecrated bag close to your altar and use its magic to boost the power of all the spells and incantations you perform.

Charm Bag to Strengthen Spells

During Samhain (Hallowe'en), craft a bag of purple fabric and fill it with two teaspoons of dried St. John's wort, a crystal of sardonix, an emblem with the solar symbol on it or a small piece of gold in the form of the Sun, and an amulet or talisman in the shape of a unicorn. Wear this bag around your neck or on your hip while performing rituals and spells.

Charm Bag to Strengthen Group Power

For those who practice group magic, this charm bag will strengthen all your charms and spells. Craft a small blue pouch and fill it with a piece of amber; an onyx; a piece of "tiger's eye;" a piece of coral, dried saffron, jasmine, and oak; dried chamomile flowers; a carved image of an owl; a magnet; a verbena root; and a lock of hair from each of the members of the coven or group. Close the bag and scent it with essential oils of saffron, camphor, and clove. At twilight on the night of the Full Moon in September, light one silver candle, one gold candle, and a white candle for each member of the group or coven. Place the bag in the center of your altar and tell it, out loud, all your magical wishes. When the flame of the last candle dies, have each·member place the bag over his or her heart for a few seconds, then set the bag aside. Each time the group performs a spell, place the bag back on the altar.

Mental Skills and Acuity

If you want to stimulate and increase your learning ability, improve your ability to retain information and your powers of concentration, or to strengthen your memory, these charm bags can help. If you find it difficult to maintain concentration during long hours of study or research, endless grueling work meetings, or tedious academic projects, they can channel the strength and concentration you need and help you maintain your alertness as long as possible.

Charm Bag to Strengthen Mind and Memory

Craft a violet bag and fill it with a small amethyst, a piece of "tiger's eye," a small piece of sandalwood, and one tablespoon of allspice. Consecrate the bag on your altar using one of the consecration rituals given in chapter 6.

Charm Bag to Open the Mind

In a blue or water-green cloth bag, place four freshly cut sprigs of rosemary, ten leaves of peppermint, three tablespoons of thyme, a teaspoon of white rice, and a piece of quartz. Consecrate the bag using one of the rituals given in chapter 6 and carry it with you to stimulate your mind and keep it open to new possibilities.

Charm Bag for Creativity I

If, for some reason, you seem to lack creativity and imagination in certain situations or need more of it in your day-to-day life, use this charm bag to channel inspirational magic. This bag is particularly useful for painters, publicists, designers, illustrators, or anyone who relies on their ability to be creative.

In a piece of purple cloth, wrap nine bay leaves, a piece of silver or a silver coin or medal, and a small drawing of the Sun made with gold ink on red paper or cloth. These elements symbolize the nine inspirational muses of Greek mythology, their mother (Mnemosyne, the goddess of memory), and Apollo, the god of poets and artists who protects the muses. Consecrate this bag on a Sunday (the day ruled by the Sun) using an essential oil with a floral aroma. Roll the piece of fabric with the elements in it and tie it with gold ribbon, making several knots around it. Take this pouch with you in your wallet or personal portfolio to channel creativity and inspire the presence of the muses.

Charm Bag for Creativity II

Craft a yellow or orange bag on a Wednesday and fill it with a piece of agate and some dried valerian root. Consecrate it on your altar using one of the rituals given in chapter 6.

Charm Bag to Improve Focus

In a blue cloth bag, put a teaspoon of dried juniper berries, a tablespoon of ginger, and a tablespoon of cinnamon. Consecrate it on your altar using one of the rituals given in chapter 6.

Charm Bag for Mental Clarity

Fill an orange cloth bag with dried jasmine and dandelion flowers, a teaspoon of rosemary, a teaspoon of chamomile, some drops of white lily or rose oil, and the top button of a shirt you particularly like.

Charm Bag to Support Meditation

Craft a blue bag and, in it, place a piece of ruffe or hematite (better known as "the glass of good luck"), a teaspoon of flax seeds, a tablespoon of grated lemon peel, and a tablespoon of melissa.

Clairvoyance and Psychic Powers

These charm bags contain various elements that can help you develop clairvoyance, seership, clairaudience, psychokinesis, and all forms of psychic manifestation. Use them to supplement your divination and psychic sessions. They will bring you natural energy and open your eyes a little more.

These charm bags are best suited to divination sessions done at home or outdoors. They can stimulate the development of prophetic dreams and prevent all kinds of psychic attacks. They can also simply help you better understand your own personal empathic qualities.

Charm Bag for Divination

In the evening hours prior to the Full Moon, place a brown square cloth on your altar. In the center of the cloth, place mustard, papaya, watermelon, and melon seeds, two cayenne flowers, and leaves from a money plant. Tie the four corners of the fabric with another piece of the brown fabric to create a sealed bag, then fully close it with a yellow or orange cloth ribbon. Scent the sack with lily and jasmine essential oils and place it next to you every time you perform a divination ritual, or rub it on your forehead several times before bedtime.

Charm Bag to Strengthen the Psyche

On the night of a New Moon, fill a dark-blue or indigo cloth bag with equal parts of sage, basil, mint, camphor, vanilla, and thyme, and a piece of a gem associated with your astrological sign. Perfume the bag with vetiver or sage oil after you have consecrated it. This talisman is perfect for all kinds of meditation and psychic work.

Charm Bag to Invoke Ancestors

Use this bag to strengthen séance sessions that invoke your ancestors. On the night of the Full Moon in November, craft a small purple bag from felt cloth and fill it with equal parts of sage, cedar, apple, and mandrake. Perfume the bag with scents of peppermint and spearmint and hang it from a blue or purple cord. Wear it around your neck during spiritual sessions.

Charm Bag for Clairvoyance

On the night of a Full Moon, pick catnip herb and dry some root of laurel. Place these in a white cloth bag. Add pine needles, an amulet shaped like an Egyptian ankh, dry powdered mandrake root, and a tulip bulb. Consecrate the bag using one of the rituals given in chapter 6 and rub it on your head every night before bed or after meditating.

Charm Bag to Strengthen the Psyche

People who work with psychic energies can use this simple charm bag to enhance their powers. Craft a silver or purple cloth bag and fill it with two teaspoons of ground dried mugwort, a teaspoon of saffron and lemon balm, a garnet, and a piece of amber. Carry the bag with you to strengthen your psyche.

Charm Bag to Strengthen Meditative and Spiritual Forces

On a Monday when the Moon is at its peak, fill a white cloth bag with lotus blossoms, white rose petals, and a few drops of oil of jasmine, lilac, or violet.

Chapter 18

Harnessing the Zodiac

The charm bags in this chapter will help channel and align the energy of your zodiac sign and attract its beneficial powers.

The Sun in the Zodiac Signs

Here is a list of twelve amulets that correspond to each of the twelve signs of the traditional zodiac. Although there are a total of eighty-eight constellations in the firmament, only fourteen of them are used to make up the zodiac. This includes Ophiuchus and Cetus, which, for various technical reasons, are not used in our Western tradition. Thus, there are only twelve signs that make up the conventional zodiac used by most Westerners today.

Each of these amulets utilizes a number of different elements that correspond to the energies of each astrological sign, drawing on their different aspects and qualities. Somewhere in this list is the right one for you. I recommend that you start by crafting your own Sun amulet and carry it around with you. Be sure not to use an amulet that corresponds to a zodiac sign that is not your own. But you can craft amulets for friends and family that correspond to their own zodiacal signs.

Fire Signs

The Fire signs of the zodiac are Aries (the Ram), Leo (the Lion), and Sagittarius (the Centaur or the Archer). These signs have elemental connections to Fire and influence personality and character traits associated with that element.

Aries (The Ram)

Those born under Aries are adventurous, energetic, rebellious, warm, cheerful, and very honest and candid. But they can also be quite impulsive. Amulets for those born under this sign will therefore channel powerful forces for protection.

When the April Full Moon reaches its highest point in the sky, light a red candle. Purchase or make an amulet in the shape or symbol of Aries and anoint it with a few drops of walnut, cedar, and olive oil. Place it on a mirror on a window sill or anywhere where the Moon is visible. The next morning, take it with you to protect you from accidents and lawsuits.

Leo (The Lion)

Leos are generous, noble, loyal, and strong. They are natural leaders and are creative, enthusiastic, and authoritarian. They generally possess great character. But those born under Leo must maintain a good career that ensures a steady income and benefits that provide some comfort. To achieve this, they need to control their pride and calm down.

To create an amulet for someone born in Leo, purchase or craft a figure in the shape of a lion or with the Leo symbol on it. Anoint the figure with a few drops of lavender oil and hold it in both hands while you visualize all the problems you normally have at work or the difficulties you may have generating income. In a corner of your bedroom, light a red candle and an incense cone beside a glass of water. Place the anointed figure in the glass of water until the next morning. Kept hidden by your bed, this amulet will enhance your powers every night while you sleep.

Sagittarius (The Centaur, The Archer)

Those born under this sign are optimistic, liberal, cheerful, friendly, curious, kind, adventurous, and impatient. But they can also be somewhat fickle—although honest. For Sagittarians, I recommend this special amulet that helps them get the forces and resources they need to succeed and fulfill their personal and financial goals.

Before the December Full Moon lights up the night, fill a glass bowl with twelve gems or glass spheres, twelve metal rings, twelve small pieces of white or crystal quartz, and a small compass. Light four blue candles around the bowl and four incense sticks of tuberose, violet, or orange. When the last candle has burned down completely, place the remaining wax and incense ashes in a grinder or mortar. Crush them together and spray the resulting powder around your front door. Keep the bowl with the crystals near your front door, or use it as a centerpiece so that all your projects meet with success.

Earth Signs

The Earth signs of the zodiac are Taurus (the Bull), Virgo (the Maiden), and Capricorn (the Goat). These signs have elemental connections to Earth and influence personality and character traits associated with that element.

Taurus (The Bull)

People born under Taurus are usually very patient, emotional, formal, affectionate, reliable, calm, and steady. But they can also be somewhat stubborn and inflexible. They therefore need a spell that can strengthen their personality and improve their presence anywhere.

Buy or craft an amulet in the shape of a bull or with the zodiacal sign of Taurus on it. Rub it with essential oil of orange and pass it through the smoke of sandalwood incense seven times, drawing circles in the air as you do so. Cover it with a piece of green felt and seal it up completely. Then bury the pouch in a pot with plants in your own bedroom or in a window of your house.

Virgo (The Maiden)

Virgos have very logical and rational minds. They are very demanding of themselves, honest, modest, shy, and hypercritical. They are usually very conservative and tend to be perfectionists. But it is often difficult for them to avoid envious people and they can sometimes absorb their negative energy. Virgos need an amulet to open pathways and remove obstacles.

On the night of the Full Moon in September, make a small amulet in the shape of a maiden. You can also use a medal or gem that has the zodiac sign of Virgo incised on it. Light a yellow candle and an incense stick of lemon or orange. Place the amulet in a small pot or cup filled with dried chamomile, a few drops of olive oil, and orange and lemon essential oil. Cover with gold or yellow fabric and let it rest overnight, preferably where it is illuminated by the Full Moon. At dawn, collect the amulet and place it on your altar or on your desk near a picture of yourself so it can constantly dissipate all your problems and open pathways to you.

Capricorn (The Goat)

Capricorns are usually very reliable, quiet, honest, loyal, persistent, ambitious, and prudent. But they can also be stubborn and grouchy. For those born under this sign, the January Full Moon has special powers. This is the time for them to perform protection rituals and magic to achieve their goals.

Buy or draw a small picture of the sign of the goat or the zodiac sign for Capricorn. This can also be carved on a rock or drawn on parchment. Light a brown or black candle to dispel all obstacles and concerns. Pour a few drops of the candle wax onto the amulet, then wrap it with black felt, tie the cloth closed, and put it in your wallet or purse. This amulet will give you magical power and ward off any problems that may hinder your projects.

Air Signs

The Air signs of the zodiac are Gemini (the Twins), Libra (the Balance), and Aquarius (the Amphora). These signs have elemental connections to Air and influence personality and character traits associated with that element.

Gemini (The Twins)

Geminis are resourceful, creative, versatile, adaptable, communicative, flexible, and impatient. But they can also be somewhat nervous and ambiguous. For those born under this sign, it is often difficult to be accepted into a group. Geminis stand out as being particularly clever, but they can also be arrogant.

On the night of the Full Moon in June, light a green candle and burn an incense stick of your favorite fragrance. Fill a crystal goblet with essential oil of calendula or mint and add a drop of your personal perfume. Add a piece of topaz or turquoise and an amulet or small figure symbolizing twins or bearing the Gemini sign. Let the goblet and its contents stand overnight, stirring it every two to five hours. At dawn, empty the cup and place the amulet in your wallet or pocket. Carry it with you every day.

Libra (The Balance)

Libras are idealistic, reserved, romantic, balanced, fair, persuasive, sociable, and kind. But they can also be easily influenced. For those born under this sign, I recommend an amulet to attract health and money.

Buy a small scale in a store, preferably one made from gold or silver. Set it on a white plate and place the plate on your magic altar or on a piece of furniture in your house that no one else touches. In a cup, mix equal parts of essences of moss, hyacinth, and rose, and anoint the scale with the mixture. On one side of the balance, place some laurel leaves; on the other, place a silver coin. Light a stick of rose or jasmine incense and keep the scale near it. This will attract health and wealth, and will keep debt collectors away.

Aquarius (The Amphora)

The children of Aquarius are remarkably friendly, liberal and social, independent, humanitarian, and individualistic. But they can also be somewhat eccentric. The Full Moon has special attributes for those born under this sign—attributes they can use better than anyone else. Aquarians need a powerful amulet that will help them make good decisions and dispel their doubts.

On the night of the Full Moon in February, buy or make an amulet or talisman in the shape of the Aquarius zodiac sign. You can also draw a picture of the sign. Light a blue candle and a white candle. Pass the amulet clockwise over the flame of both candles. Then place the amulet in a bowl filled with clean water and leave it there until the candles burn down completely. As they burn, visualize the water as a sponge sucking all your doubts and uncertainties out of the amulet. When the candles are completely burned down, remove the amulet and place it in a visible place in your bedroom. Make sure you put it somewhere you can find it easily whenever you are in doubt about a decision you have to make.

Water Signs

The Water signs of the zodiac are Cancer (the Crab), Scorpio (the Scorpion), and Pisces (the Fish). These signs have elemental connections to Water and influence personality and character traits associated with that element.

Cancer (The Crab)

People born under this sign are highly emotional, persevering, cautious, very sensitive, easy to impress, and sometimes melancholy. But, to a lesser extent, they can also be capricious and irritable. For those born under Cancer, I suggest an amulet to increase concentration and the willingness to work or study.

In July, preferably under a Full Moon, light a vanilla- or fruit-scented candle. Make an amulet in the shape of a crab or the zodiac sign for Cancer. Anoint it with seven drops of rosehip oil or amber extract. Hold the amulet with both hands for a few minutes, concentrating on your long-term desires, then place it under your pillow. Every Full Moon, anoint it with seven more drops of oil before you go to sleep to renew its power.

Scorpio (The Scorpion)

Scorpios are tenacious, willful, loyal, passionate, kind, curious, and intuitive. But they can also be very reserved and somewhat stubborn. They need a special charm to harness the positive energies of their sign.

Buy a figure of a scorpion or make one from any material of your choice. You can also use a gem with the astrological symbol of Scorpio engraved on it. Place the figure in a glass bowl and add a tablespoon of each of the following essences: tuberose, moss, rose, and cedar. Cover the bowl with a white cloth and place it in the light of the Full Moon in November. Retrieve it the next day. This amulet will avert misfortunes, anxieties, and negative influences.

Pisces (The Fish)

Pisces are humble and hardworking and have a very good sense of humor. They are also creative, sensitive, intuitive, and kind and tend to have great spiritual sensitivity. But those born under Pisces may need to balance their time and their lives to keep them under control.

Craft this amulet during the March Full Moon. Fill a small bowl with equal parts of water, musk oil, and rose water. Add a gem or charm that has the sign of Pisces engraved or drawn on it. Light a dark-blue or indigo candle and place the bowl next to it. Let the candle burn down completely. At dawn, remove the amulet from the bowl and leave it to dry in a high place during the day beside a jasmine incense stick. Carry this amulet with you everywhere to improve your quality of life.

The Moon in the Zodiac Signs

The Moon exerts remarkable power over the Earth. It influences dreams, tides, emotions, animals, plants, and even our own understanding of time. Although its light is a reflection of the light from our star, the Sun, the Moon takes over the Sun's energies and strengthens and perfects them before reflecting them back to us. Just as a prism splits white light into a variety of colors, the Moon converts sunlight into something more influential and varied. Lunar cycles also affect various forms of sorcery

The Moon has enormous power over Nature. It governs fertility, plant growth, ocean waves, and animal behavior, as well as the way we perceive all these things. It especially rules all night creatures—owls, spiders, the Queen of the Night flower, and even the witches who stroll among the trees at midnight picking sage and mandrake guided by the light of the Silver Mother. This beautiful round rock orbiting in space is just the right distance from the Earth to influence all of its processes—a faithful and noble companion who was there long before mankind understood her meaning and gave her a name. Physics tells us that the closer two objects are, the greater the force that draws them together will be and the greater the mutual influence between them. The gravitational pull of the Moon influences the movements of the ocean and its constant waves, and, in turn, all marine life and its evolution.

The Moon also influences our health and especially the diets we eat. According to popular belief, diets tend to be more effective during the waning Moon, which is related to increased physical activity and energy drain. The Full Moon, on the other hand, urges us to consume plenty of fluids and nutrients to restore our health. During the New Moon, the body does its best to detoxify and free itself from unnecessary substances. During the Crescent Moon, diets that help us gain weight are most effective. This is also the Moon phase in which we feel a greater energy reserve in our bodies.

In European folklore, the Moon is associated with epileptic seizures and internal bleeding. Its influence is closely linked to female cycles of menstruation, pregnancy, and childbirth, as well as to the growth and maturity of men. The lunar cycle and the female menstrual cycle are intimately and uniquely connected to each other. Both last for approximately twenty-eight days. The Moon disappears from view for three nights (at the start of the New Moon), and returns in its full glory on the fourteenth day of its cycle, when it appears as a Full Moon illuminating the sky. Likewise, the twenty-eight-day female menstrual cycle results in ovulation on the fourteenth day.

The Moon also governs our emotions and the decisions we make. Women seem to become more sensitive and perhaps more vulnerable during periods close to the Full Moon, while men tend to feel more emotional during a Crescent Moon. The decisions made during the Full Moon tend to lead to quick results and be more effective. Moreover, the Full Moon is also the most suitable time for planting trees, conducting negotiations, making associations, and gambling.

In South America, it is quite common to find shops and salons that offer beauty treatments based on the lunar phases. Facials, cream baths, and treatments for hair loss are undertaken during the waning Moon, while hair coloring and curling treatments are applied during the Crescent Moon. Firming massages are recommended during the waxing Moon, while skin hydration and body treatments are given during the New Moon. Haircuts, on the other hand, are more successful during the Full Moon and promise to make the hair grow strong, healthy, and abundant.

Here are twelve charm bags that can help you channel the power of the Moon through its associations with the twelve astrological signs. You can craft all of the following bags for your own use, or for friends or family, but they can only be crafted when the Moon is in the sign of the person who will use them. There are astrological calendars and mobile apps that can show you which sign the Moon will be in on specific dates.

Fire Signs

When the Moon is in the Fire signs, it is the ideal time for magic that involves the Fire element—Sun and light. The Fire signs give you power through the Moon. Use that power for spells that feed passion and inspire greatness.

Aries ♈

When the Moon is in the astrological sign of the Ram, this is the best time for charm bags that channel courage and personal freedom, overcome personal challenges, invigorate all aspects of physical energy, and increase enthusiasm and the desire to live. It's the right time for protection spells involving wisdom, intuitive development, and personal energy and self-confidence. It is also propitious for healing rituals and for increasing your power to fight fury and injustice.

On a night with the Moon in Aries, light a red candle to symbolize Fire and a stick of herbal incense. Fill a red cloth bag with equal parts of raspberries and/or sun-dried strawberries, natural cotton (unprocessed), and a small image or symbol of a ram. You can scent the bag before sealing it fully by applying a few drops of essential oil of basil and peridot.

Leo ♌

When the Moon is in the astrological sign of the Lion, it is the best time for rituals that channel and stimulate intuition, leadership, respect, teamwork, the admiration of others, generosity, creativity, and prestige. This is the right time to perform magic related to your physical body. The Moon in Leo can help athletes achieve better results. It is a propitious time to do magic to gain strength and endurance and to protect yourself from accidents, sprains, and muscle tears.

On a night when the Moon is in the sign of Leo, light a red candle to symbolize Fire and a stick of herbal incense. Fill a red cloth bag with equal parts of rue and St. John's wort, then add a small image or symbol of a lion or a piece of gold. You can scent the charm bag before sealing it fully by applying a few drops of essential oil of angelica.

Sagittarius ♐

As the Moon transits the astrological sign of the Archer, the time is favorable for performing rituals and consecrating charm bags that channel and somehow strengthen your independence and communication skills. This is the best time for attracting sympathy, honesty, joy of life, spontaneity, eloquence, and self-respect. It is a propitious time to perform magic that furthers your projects and goals and magic related to optimism and enthusiasm. The Moon in Sagittarius supports spells to protect against theft and weapons and to achieve independence, courage, and freedom, as well as incantations that strengthen your talents and skills and rituals for achieving success and dispelling fear.

On a night when the Moon is in the sign of Sagittarius, light a red candle symbolizing Fire and a stick of herbal incense. Fill a red cloth bag with equal parts of dried root of malt and rose petals, then add a small image or symbol of an arrow or the tip of an actual arrow. You can even add a piece of jasper. You can scent the charm bag before sealing it fully by applying a few drops of essential oil of violets.

Earth Signs

When the Moon is in the Earth signs, it is the ideal time for magic that involves the Earth element, Nature, and plants. The Moon in the Earth signs gives you the power to cast spells that promote will and sympathy.

Taurus ♉

The Moon in the astrological sign of the Bull is the best time for charm bags consecrated to finding items and to stimulating talents considered lost. This Moon encourages patience, as well as the courage to act against unfair rules. It is the best time to bless charm bags that attract modesty and humility, as well as to strengthen self-analysis, personal and family introspection, and the development of common sense. This is the best time to perform magic related to self-control and will, spells that involve making decisions and changes, and rituals to enhance your competitive spirit. This Moon also supports rituals to balance the personality and make good use of free time, as well as those that promote the healing of physical and mental ailments. The Moon in Taurus also encourages the development of ideas and projects.

On a night when the Moon is in Taurus, light a green candle to symbolize Earth and a stick of myrrh incense. Fill a green cloth bag with equal parts of mauve and dried mint, then add a figure or symbol of a bull or a cow. You can scent your charm bag before sealing it fully by applying a few drops of essential oil of ginger or roses.

Virgo ♍

As the Moon moves through the astrological sign of the Maiden, the time is most propitious for creating and consecrating charm bags that require a lot of detail and that somehow seem more laborious or complicated to you. It is the perfect time for talismans that attract willpower, constancy, and perseverance, and those that inspire interest in new and curious things. This Moon also supports charm bags that promote health and cleanse the body. The Moon in Virgo is the right time to perform magic that strengthens the senses, promotes spirituality, and dissipates doubts. It enhances magic that involves friendship and compassion, as well as spells to gain experience and overcome difficult situations. This Moon can help you find the solution to something that afflicts you and can help you drive away evil spirits

On a night when the Moon is in Virgo, light a green candle to symbolize Earth and a stick of myrrh incense. Fill a yellow fabric bag with equal parts of wild carrot or lemon peel and root of cyclamen, then add a small image or symbol of a maiden. You can scent the charm bag before sealing it fully by applying a few drops of pine or chamomile essential oil.

Capricorn ♑

When the Moon is in the sign of the Goat, it is time to craft and consecrate charm bags designed to attract (or influence) concentration, determination, ambition, loyalty, prudence, tenacity, peace, tolerance, and fidelity. This is the right time for spells related to the purchase and sale of property, for rituals to attract protection, and for magic related to astral projection. The Moon in Capricorn strengthens rituals to take care of your plants or garden and all kinds of spiritualist invocations. It can also help you move away from pessimism and depression.

On a night when the Moon is in Capricorn, light a green candle to symbolize Earth and a stick of myrrh incense. Fill a brown or dark-blue cloth bag with equal parts of elder and clove, then add a small image of a goat or a spider. You can scent the bag before sealing it fully by applying a few drops of essential oil of hyacinth or moss.

Air Signs

When the Moon is in the Air signs, it is the ideal time to create magic that involves the element of Air, the climate, and thought. The Moon in Air signs gives you power to effect change and cast spells for mental and spiritual transformation.

Gemini ♊

When the Moon transits the sign of the Twins, it is a preferred time to make charm bags that stimulate and strengthen vitality, ingenuity, and curiosity. This Moon supports communication as a form of social and personal development, as well as all amulets that protect you during travel and negotiations. The Moon in Gemini is best suited to magic related to social relations, friendship, honesty, and justice, and magic that balances your life and recovers time you've lost. It empowers emotional healings and makes the cooking of healing beverages or formulas more effective. This is the Moon of the alchemists, who used her power to manifest the transmutation of metals.

On a night when the Moon is in Gemini, light a yellow candle to symbolize Air and an incense stick of mauve or jasmine. Fill a white or yellow cloth bag with equal parts of ginger and fresh mint, then add a small image or symbol of twins or a dove. You can scent the bag before sealing it fully by applying a few drops of essential oil of acacia or vanilla.

Libra ♎

There is no better time than the lunar transit of the sign of the Balance for making charm bags designed to bring equilibrium to every aspect of your life. The Moon in Libra is suitable for all magic that attracts equilibrium, justice, eloquence, and protection from vengeful or spiteful people. This is the time for rituals to balance your life and your thoughts, to drive away sorrows, and to forget bad experiences. This Moon promotes the learning of a new science and the development of magical abilities to control the spirits. Its magic is related to longevity and youth, as well as to healing someone who is far away.

On a night when the Moon is in Libra, light a white or light-blue candle to symbolize Air and a stick of jasmine incense. Craft a cloth bag of the same color as the candle and fill it with equal parts of oats and catnip, then add a small image or symbol of a scale. You can scent the charm bag before sealing it fully by applying a few drops of hyacinth or gladiolus essential oil.

Aquarius ♒

When the Moon is in the sign of the Amphora, or the "cup-bearer of heaven," it is the best time for magic related to social and humanitarian aid, including charm bags to help others and to bring peace and solidarity. It also brings important powers to charm bags intended to encourage creativity, inspiration, original-ity, and the development of strategies of all kinds. There's no better time for climate-related spells than this Moon. The Celts believed that the Moon in Aquarius has the power to bring rain in times of drought. Moreover, the rain that falls during this Moon's waning is considered quite special. This is the right Moon to get you out of a jam or a complicated situation. Under its light, craft charm bags to strengthen courage and return hope to a beloved one.

On a night when the Moon is in Aquarius, light a yellow candle to symbolize the wind and Air, and a stick of jasmine incense. Fill a bag of light-green or blue fabric with equal parts of angelica and myrrh, then add a small image or symbol of a dolphin or an amphora. You can scent the charm bag before sealing it fully by applying a few drops of essential oil of lily.

Water Signs

When the Moon is in the Water signs, it is right time for magic involving the Water element, intuition, and changes. Water signs help you effect all kinds of transmutations; they support physical healing, develop clairvoyance, and strengthen the psyche.

Cancer ♋

When the Moon transits the sign of the Crab, it is the right time to make and consecrate charm bags designed to stimulate psychic abilities, clairvoyance, and precognition, and to contact the spiritual realm. It is also a great time for charm bags that channel fertility, virility, sexuality, conception, motherhood and fatherhood, and affection and respect in a couple. This Moon is favorable for strengthening the qualities of expression on both artistic and psychic levels and has remarkable healing power. The Full Moon in the sign of Cancer is the most suitable time for magic that strengthens bones and the immune system, and for magic to overcome obstacles and prevent threats.

On a night when the Moon is in Cancer, light a blue candle to symbolize Water and a stick of incense with a fruity aroma. Fill a gray cloth bag with equal parts of rosehip, acacia, and lime, then add a small image or symbol of a crab. You can scent the charm bag before sealing it fully by applying a few drops of essential oil of amber.

Scorpio ♏

When the Moon is in the sign of the Scorpion, it is a great time for charm bags that channel energies linked to sensitivity and emotional depth and to memories of the past. This is a good time to heal emotional wounds, perform regressions, and study your incarnations and past lives. This Moon strengthens magic that reveals secrets and spells designed to find things. It also supports rituals related to passion and the most intense emotions. Use the power of the Moon in Scorpio to combat apathy, improve your mood, and fight depression. The Full Moon in Scorpio is the night when the Druids prepared brews to protect against poisons. In certain traditions, it is the best night to make love potions and perform spells related to nobility and intuition.

On a night when the Moon is in Scorpio, light a blue candle to symbolize Water and a stick of incense with a fruity aroma. Fill an indigo cloth bag with equal parts of nettle, sage, and mugwort, then add a small image or symbol of a scorpion. You can scent the charm bag before sealing it fully by applying a few drops of essential oil of tuberose and musk oil.

Pisces ♓

As the Moon transits the sign of the Fish, charm bags linked to control acquire a special force. This Moon helps strengthen and counteract different emotions and stimulates love of the arts. It also helps you appreciate your own artistic skills and talents. This is the Moon for making charm bags that fight fear, confusion, and instability. Wiccans favor this Moon for practicing *feng shui*. It is the Moon of absolute transmutation, for making all kinds of changes in your life. Whether you seek physical or material change or a change of residence or place of work or even if you seek to alter your personality for the better, this Moon can help. It is the Moon of constant balance, whose powers can help you regain your own equilibrium and give you control over your life despite situations that may arise.

On a night when the Moon is in Pisces, light a blue candle to symbolize the ocean and the Water element, and a stick of incense with a fruity aroma. Fill a blue cloth bag with equal parts of fennel, jasmine, sandalwood, and sage, then add a small image or symbol of one or two fish. You can scent the charm bag before sealing it fully by applying a few drops of essential oil of orange blossom.

Celebrating the Calendar

The charm bags in this section are made on special days of the calendar year because they make use of the unique energies of those days.

Charm Bag for Walpurgis Night

To celebrate the magical night of Walpurgis, it is customary in different parts of the world to burn fragrant incense in the corners of the home, visit the forest, summon the gods of fertility, and prepare homemade bread. Some traditions include an extensive celebration on Walpurgis night itself, followed by one on Beltane, the next day. Channeling the magical powers of this day can help you move between the astral and the physical planes.

To channel the powers of this day, make a yellow or orange charm bag and fill it with a piece of red jasper, a piece of heliotrope, and a piece of amber. Add some mint and eucalyptus leaves, a tablespoon of dry powdered ginger, and a bracelet handmade from herbs and flowers that you picked in a nearby park. This symbolizes your magical bond with Mother Nature. Consecrate this charm bag several days before the celebration and carry it with you to it. It will help you channel the transitional energies of the day, giving you the power to move between planes. It also stimulates your capacity to perform astral projection and allows you to move freely between the dream world and the spiritual world.

Charm Bag for Christmas/Yule

In some countries, a special ritual is celebrated called "Invoking the Christmas Spirit"—that magical spirit that sleeps for most of the year and returns on the Winter Solstice to spread its halo of happiness and hope over the world, bring peace, and grant wishes. There are many different rituals that invoke and channel the magical presence of this spirit and bring its happiness to us. This is a charm bag that is very popular for conjuring the Christmas spirit in my country.

Perfume a green cloth bag. You can decorate the bag with a nice design if you wish. Fill the bag with nuts, cinnamon sticks, pieces of dehydrated fruit (or seeds), a piece of amethyst, and a silver coin dedicated during a Full Moon. You can also add a high-denomination bill. Consecrate the bag with a few drops of essential oil of apple, cedar, and juniper, and place it on a table on the night of the Winter Solstice, next to a green, red, or purple candle. After Christmas, set the amulet aside for the following year and consecrate it again every Winter Solstice.

Charm Bag for Abundance on Christmas/Yule

Craft a green bag with ribbons and hanging threads of green, red, and white. Fill it with half a tablespoon of pine, half a tablespoon of root or leaves of oak ground to a powder, a tablespoon of fresh mistletoe, twenty apple seeds, and a cinnamon stick. Scent the bag with a few drops of essential oil of pine and cinnamon, then bless it on your altar. On Christmas Spirit night, place it on your dining table with a green candle and thank the spirits for the favors granted.

Charm Bag for Samhain

This charm bag will help you stimulate your growth as a practitioner of magic. At the same time, it can work to augment your powers on the spiritual level, allowing you to draw new teachers and teachings to you.

Craft a brown or dark-green charm bag and fill it with juniper, white rose petals, myrrh, frankincense or lemon balm, and a gem associated with your astrological sign. Consecrate the bag inside a circle of sea salt in front of your altar on Samhain night. You can perfume it with the essential oil that corresponds to your zodiac sign, then tie it at the end with a purple ribbon. Wear this every day and see a progressive change in your various faculties associated with magic and spirituality.

Conclusion

Believe in Yourself

In popular magic, as well as in traditional witchcraft, there is a very common saying: "He who does not believe in himself, fails to believe in anyone else." This wise motto applies to everyone—in all walks of life and for all endeavors. If you do not believe in yourself, you can not expect others to do so. If you cannot challenge yourself and try to improve yourself, the world may overcome you without you even realizing it.

Whether or not you believe in the esoteric arts or mysticism, you must learn to believe in yourself. Once you realize your own potential, you can exploit it and develop it. You can evolve spiritually and take control over your everyday life. Once you believe in yourself, you realize that you can achieve all you ever dreamed of and make it manifest into reality—*your* reality.

In magic, it is an important principle that you must be able to perceive what is within your reach and what is not. But the purest truth of magic is that *everything* is at your fingertips and *nothing* is impossible. As with everything in life, however, you must work for it through diligent study and constant practice.

Practice makes perfect, that's very true. To get results, you must first try. And sometimes, you must try over and over again, otherwise your magical practice will be like buying a single lottery ticket and giving up if you lose. If you want to win, you must keep trying. And the same applies to scientific research, to spirituality, and to everything you want in life. Magic brings you a whole universe of possibilities, but if you want to realize them, you must reach for them with strong commitment and hard practice. Be ready to acknowledge this and never forget that those who persevere win.

Learn to believe in yourself and the power that dwells within you. Do not give up at your first defeat, and do not bow to disappointment. When you find yourself disheartened, take a deep breath, smile, and move forward. Magic can help you achieve all sorts of goals in your life. But you have to put your back into it; do not expect magic to do it all for you.

Honor Traditions

The world today is drowning in technological advances. And in fact, many of them are very useful. But technology tends to make people look for what they think they want in a store, instead of turning to older spiritual traditions that are as firm, steadfast, and vibrant as they were in centuries gone by. Honoring these older traditions can satisfy you, not only emotionally and spiritually, but also by bringing you into contact with your ancestors, so you can share with them and honor them by worshipping the deities and practices they followed when they were part of the world of the living.

Traditions allow you to honor the past and all who came into the world before you. But you must approach them with an honest respect and practice them from your heart. Some magical practices may seem like colorful and cheerful festivities, but others are often sad and rather nostalgic. Nonetheless, they all offer you a way to celebrate life, changes, joy, and humanity in different ways. When you study the traditions of your ancestors and your family, and when you honor them, you rediscover yourself in your own roots and your own past. And when you study the traditions of other peoples and countries and, in one way or another, become part of them, you begin to acquaint yourself with the larger world around you.

Magic and Desire

Magic is driven by desire, feeling, and memory. It is the purest expression of life in the cosmos and the universal glue of time that balances and unifies past and future in a single line to create our present—a time full of expectations and hopes for tomorrow. It is the pure soul that inhabits our existential reality. It is constantly growing and is itself an expression of the greatest force of the eternal spirit.

Witness the magic of the ripples that form on the surface of a river and transform the reflection of the Moon as you meditate on its banks. Drink in the magic of the fresh breeze, replete with exciting aromas, that envelops you as you walk through a park or past the front garden of the house of your dreams. This magic is there to grant you everything you need, and occasionally to help you get what you wish for. You just have to know how to ask, and magic can transform all your desires into reality. It can deliver the stuff of your dreams from that distant imaginary paradise to the environment around you.

Once you begin to understand the wonderful power of the magic in your life, you will be able to apply it to every aspect of your life that you may now consider beyond your control. With the energy of the entire universe in your hands, *you* can become the magical spirit in the air that you breathe, the wisdom of that good friend and counselor you rely on, and the noble confidant that keeps all your secrets.

However, magic requires both understanding and responsibility. It can help you whenever you ask it from the heart, but it will often also teach you a lesson. Sometimes, it will help you and you may not even realize it. Sometimes, you may forget to thank it for all it has done for you. But the mystical energy of magic will always be present in every corner and in every moment of your life to advise you, protect you, serve you, and guide you.

Learn how to use magic and how to live with it. Awaken the magic that is within you and channel through it the sacred future that you crave. Let yourself be guided by the pure and ancient soul of the cosmos and its eternal wisdom.

Plant some verbena. Make a wish. Consecrate an amulet. Draw a star. All this is free.

Afterword

Walking at midnight through the fog and the forest on Walpurgis night, the witch and her owl climbed the steep slope to the highest peak of the old mountain. She was on her way to meet the horned god who protects witches. She was on her way to save her beloved.

The wise woman brought with her an offering—a tribute of apples, meats, and cheeses wrapped in a blanket. Following the advice of the fortune teller in her village, she buried the bundle under the noblest tree she could find as the icy wind swirled the hoot of the owl around her.

Do not marry in May, the stories warned. Do not chop down the oak, the winds whispered. But her beloved did not listen. While he was cutting down an oak tree on the last night of April, a lady in white appeared before him and stole his heart and all his power of emotion. She looked just like all those who walk among the living during the month of May, so the beloved did not heed the warning. He married Death in the early morning of the first day of May.

The witch found herself in the heart of the forest at midnight on this night of nights—the night of witches, the darkest night of all, when the spirits awaken and empower magical spells and enchantments of all kinds. Following the tradition of the horned god, she picked sacred cascara, orange blossom, and verbena, which she ground with stones and scented with herbs. She wrapped the mixture in a sack of old cloth and tied it with her hair, making seven knots. Then she consecrated the bag to the Moon that bids farewell to the light and buried the strange talisman by the door of the home of her beloved.

The spirit of Death, disguised as a beautiful woman, cried out and went back to her world. And the witch regained the heart of the man she had always loved.

Where verbena is buried, spirits recede. Where the Moon shines, witches govern. Where Walpurgis is celebrated, no one marries. Where forests mutter, the horned god prevails.

Appendix A

Creed of the Mage

Respect the Divinity at all times and everywhere.
Seek the truth at all times and everywhere.
Follow the path, always with kindness.
Find the path, never for vanity.
Walk quietly, without disturbing others.
Learn humility, with no pretensions to others.
Empty your mind before initiation.
Do not let anything make you hesitate.
Study calmly and learn fondly.
Respect teachers who know their journey.
In the woods, collect herb and flowers.
Let your altar be graced by fairies.
Walk along the river between the shore and the bank.
Do not throw rocks; do not disturb the oak.
Learn from everyone; teach and share.
Care for the forest, which is Mother and Sire.
If in the forest you spy the fairy dance,
Beware of gnomes and elves.
If seven knots on the ribbon you perform,
Seven leprechauns will come to your door.

If sacred cascara is found when walking,
Pick it up five times and you will be healed.
On St. John's night, his wort you must find.
Burn it to the ground in order to exorcize.
Who suffers from nerves, verbena you shall give.
Who seeks clairvoyance, mugwort has to swig.
The herbalist and the shaman you must respect.
Without their wisdom, you can not improve health.
The tarantula you see, alienate you should not.
They are very often omens of good news to come.
Adore the deer and its antlers decorate.
Good fortune will come to your home
at all times and everywhere you rest.
May your altar at home be full of wreaths
To appease the spirits with flowers and herbs.
With lily and chrysanthemum, decorate your mirror.
With oils of juniper and cedar, scent you dominions.
The lady in white you should always aid
When at the crossroads crying you may find her
Collecting elderberry and basil
And burning sage looking for her son.
The witch serves the woods and you will soon know
If you ridicule the witch, for the forest will be torn.
Toast with red wine for your enemies.
Poor may those be who thwart you.
Their names three times you have burned
And karma will give them a special treat.
Find carnation; it will do you good.
Dry it in the sun and drink it brewed
To relieve pain and heal swelling.
If in the woods pathbreaking you can find,
Take it with you and it shall give you good fortune.
Rue, rosemary, and Saint John's wort

Burned in a cauldron—good luck they grant.
Draw a star in every corner and on every door.
Nothing will stop you if the five spikes you see.
If fairies in your garden you want to see,
Look for yerba santa and rub it on the temple.
If fairies are hidden and you can not see,
Embrace a nearby tree and it may intercede.
If some evil afflicts you that you can not handle,
Write it in the sand to move it away.
Greet the Sun every morning and receive his blessing.
Respect the father and the mother to receive their praise.
Say goodbye to the king every evening,
And the next day you will get his blessing.
Greet the Moon before the Sabbat
And in the coven, she will come out.
Bid farewell to the lunar cycle in its evening light
And joy will come to you in abundance.
If a witch coven does evil,
The universe will punish it.
If your faith in someone is destroyed,
Look in the woods for the dishonored one.
Although many others have they judged,
Gods and spirits are still revered
And before huge towers that want to light
The humble woods, will always live.
Be devout and always honored.
Be yourself despite what happens.
If you seek wisdom, egos you will cross.
Great sagacity is granted by the Gods.

Appendix B

Plant, Flower, and Gemstone Magic

Plants, herbs, flowers, and gemstones of all kinds have specific powers and energies that can be called on in magic and in holistic and alternative therapies. Some of these influences are associated with elemental forces; some are associated with zodiacal rulership. Here is a summary of the most common plants and gemstones used in crafting charm bags to harness these energies.

Plants for the Signs of the Zodiac

- **Aries**: basil, honeysuckle, poppy seed, red cayenne

- **Leo**: laurel, rough, saffron, sunflower, Trinidadian

- **Sagittarius**: borage, cinnamon, gladioli, salvia

- **Taurus**: clove, dahlia, lily, mint, poppy

- **Virgo**: daisy, hazel, hyacinth, impatiens, lavender

- **Capricorn**: gardenia, ginger, lily, oak, tulip, vanilla

- **Gemini**: anise, chrysanthemum, lily of the valley, marjoram

- **Libra**: hydrangea, jasmine, linden, poplar, violet

- *Aquarius*: bird of paradise, daffodil, orchid

- *Cancer*: geranium, lily, magnolia

- *Scorpio*: bromeliad, eucalyptus, lotus, mustard seed

- *Pisces*: aquatic algae, calla lily, pink rose, water lily

Plants with Magical Energies

- *Aphrodisiac*: cinnamon, clove, ginseng, oak, saffron, vanilla

- *Divination and fortune-telling*: artemisia, birch, clove, garlic, hazel, heather, henbane, mandrake

- *Enchantment*: anise, heather, henbane, mandrake, marjoram, mistletoe, rosemary, rue

- *Freedom and independence*: alfalfa, fir, holly, mint

- *Friendship*: calendula, chamomile, eucalyptus, hyacinth, lily, rose, tangerine, violet

- *Good fortune*: acacia, clover, holly, mint, oak, poppy, rosemary

- *Happiness*: burdock, chicory, clover, mistletoe, rue, saffron, St. John's wort

- *Health*: clove, coriander, honeysuckle, salvia, saffron, thyme

- *Inspiration and creativity*: hazel, laurel, vid

- *Intuition and clairvoyance*: artemisia, basil, ginseng, hazel, mint, salvia

- *Invocation*: alder, anise, artemisia, heather, henbane, jasmine, mustard, thyme, vervain, vid

- *Love*: acacia, basil, cinnamon, clove, coriander, chamomile, jasmine, juniper, lavender, rose

- *Money and wealth*: acacia, almond, basil, cinnamon, clove, jasmine, mint, sandalwood

- *Peace*: chamomile, lily, rose, rue

- *Protection*: acacia, basil, clover, garlic, jasmine, juniper, oak, tangerine, thyme, salvia, sandalwood, St. John's wort

- *Psychic power*: arnica, artemisa, eucalyptus, geranium, hazel, heather, mandrake, marjoram

- *Purification*: cedar, garlic, jasmine, laurel, mandrake, sandalwood, vervain

- *Spirituality*: geranium, holly, mandrake, marjoram, rue

- *Value*: almond, bryonia, cherry tree, chicory, garlic, ginseng

- *Wisdom*: almond, artemisia, eucalyptus, hazel, rosemary, salvia, vanilla

Gemstones for the Signs of the Zodiac

- *Aries*: pyrite, ruby, sapphire

- *Leo*: amber, diamond, red jasper, ruby

- *Sagittarius*: amethyst, turquoise

- *Taurus*: emerald, green jade, pink coral

- *Virgo*: blue agate, malachite, peridot

- *Capricorn*: black opal, jet, onyx

- *Gemini*: agate, cat's eye, topaz

- *Libra*: green jade, pink quartz, sapphire

- *Aquarius*: indigo sapphire, lapis lazuli
- *Cancer*: moonstone, pearl, quartz, silver
- *Scorpio*: garnet, opal, smoky quartz
- *Pisces*: aquamarine, coral, jade, pearl

Appendix C

Weekday Magic

Each day of the week has different energetic qualities that can be associated with different forms of magic. If you use this magical principle to guide your rituals, spells, and charms, you can make them more effective by linking them to a much higher energy.

Monday

Mondays are associated with the Moon. This is the right day to perform magic that affects your tranquility, calm, and inner peace, as well as your awareness, sensitivity, and intuition. The Moon governs intuition, spirituality, feelings, Nature, and time. Magic linked to it also helps you dispel sadness and fear.

Monday is an excellent day for all divinations and rituals that strengthen clairvoyance or psychic powers. It is a good time to contact the astral plane or the world of the dead and to perform all sorts of magical work associated with spirituality or dispelling fear and sorrow.

Rituals performed with white, silver, or gray candles linked to the Moon take on a greater power when performed on a Monday. The recommended incense for this day is jasmine. Silver and labradorite are perfect gems and metals to bless on a Monday.

Tuesday

Tuesdays are ruled by the planet Mars. It is the right day to perform magic that affects deep-rooted emotions like passion, courage, anger, and resentment. It is a great day for rituals whose function is to strengthen positive aspects of yourself or to perform magic for protection.

Mars rules passions, strength, strategy, war, and fighting. The magic linked to Mars helps you overcome negative feelings and placate thoughts of disgust or revenge. Tuesday is a wonderful day for all kinds of amulets, talismans, and magical charms that protect you and your loved ones from envy, jealousy, betrayal, and teasing. It is a good day for dispelling evil influences and for warding off your enemies or any entity that tries to harm you.

Tuesdays are recommended for rituals that are performed with red, white, and black candles, or those linked to the mystic and warrior energy of Mars. Suggested incense for this day is orange or lemon. It is also an excellent day for blessing iron implements for protection.

Wednesday

Wednesday is ruled by the planet Mercury. It is the right day to perform magic linked to communication, travel, trade, wisdom, mastery of other languages, and magical healing. Mercury rules trade, economy, travel, languages, and knowledge related to other cultures. The magic linked to Mercury can also help you resolve a problem or escape a situation in which you feel trapped.

Wednesday is a great day to perform spells and rituals that grant wishes, facilitate travel, bring raises and promotions, and advance the economy. It empowers all kinds of magic related to income, prosperity, and abundance. It is also a good day for rituals that involve pursuing a better job or seeking a raise in your present position.

Rituals performed with yellow, green, and brown candles, or magic related to communication and spontaneity are more powerful on a Wednesday, because these represent Mercury. The recommended incense for this day is copal or coral. Pieces of agate blessed on a Wednesday become more powerful than those blessed on any other day.

Thursday

Thursdays are associated with Jupiter. This is the right day for magic that influences money, generosity, prosperity, greatness, justice, loyalty, and honor. Jupiter rules over happiness, prosperity, success, recognition, and wealth. The magic linked to Jupiter helps you make difficult decisions calmly and precisely.

Thursday is an excellent day to perform rituals and spells that improve every aspect of your life—economic, personal, family, spiritual, and even health. This day also grants more power to spells linked to virility, good luck, legal affairs, and riches.

Thursday strengthens rituals performed with green, dark-red, and purple candles, or candles that are linked to the magical influence of Jupiter. The recommended incense for this day is cedar or roses. Sapphire and tin charge with much more power when blessed on this day.

Friday

Fridays are under the influence of Venus. This is the right day to perform magic that influences love, friendship, beauty, joy, purity, honesty, and general happiness. Venus rules over positive and warm feelings, love, friendship, and inner well-being, as well as external beauty, fertility, and femininity. The magic linked to Venus has the power to placate past loves and to keep away unwanted lovers.

Friday is a wonderful day for magic that positively influences the heart and the feelings of someone specific. Rituals linked to love, passion, sexuality, and fertility are more powerful on a Friday, as well as amulets that protect your loved ones.

On Friday, magical rituals performed with white, red, and pink candles become highly effective, as do all spells somehow linked with the planet Venus. The recommended incense for this day is jasmine, rose, or lavender. Fridays are suitable for blessing copper, emeralds, and rose quartz.

Saturday

Saturday is associated with Saturn. It is the proper day for spells and rituals involving longevity, family unity, renewal, the warmth of home, and changes. Saturn rules over agriculture, crops, and fields, as well as life in all its forms. The magic linked to Saturn has the power to thwart your worst enemies and prolong life.

Saturday is a good day to study and implement formulas and magical works related to life and death, renewal, meditation, and reincarnation. It is also a great day to carry out magic that nullifies or completely neutralizes negative forces, dark entities, and bad vices.

On Saturday, rituals performed with brown, gray, black, and blue candles gain great strength. This is true for all works involving the planet Saturn. It is a good day to burn myrrh or incense with an herbal aroma. Lead, black jet, and opal are suitable for any type of blessing on this day.

Sunday

Sunday is governed by the Sun. It is the best day to perform magic linked in some way to divine ascension, to improve health, to strengthen spirituality, and to protect against all evil. The Sun rules over material prosperity, success, personal triumph, and magic in its most spiritual form. Magic linked to the Sun allows you to get closer to divinity and to achieve spiritual elevation.

Sunday is an excellent day for celebrations and rituals linked to personal achievement, goals achieved, and the worship of different deities in a variety of pantheons. It is a day of great energetic power for strengthening spells that attract wealth and help you achieve short- and long-term goals.

On Sundays, rituals performed with yellow, orange, and gold candles, or those linked to the energy of the Sun, become much more powerful. The recommended incense for this day is bay or vervain. Sunday is the recommended day to bless pieces of gold and/or diamonds.

Appendix D

Incense Magic

Below is a list of the incenses most commonly used in witchcraft. You can use them to cleanse the atmosphere of your home, bless your altar, and consecrate your charm bags. They are also effective in divination sessions.

The first list gives the incenses alphabetically, along with their attributes. The second gives the attributes alphabetically, followed by specific incenses. The third gives the zodiac signs with their associated incenses, and the last gives the days of the week and their corresponding fragrances. This will help you better determine which incense is most appropriate for your magical purposes.

Incenses by Attribute

- **Almond**: Cleanses negative energies of all kinds from personal items, clothing, and jewelry; also has aphrodisiac properties.

- **Aloe vera**: Attracts calm and tranquility; use to consecrate charm bags tied to money and material prosperity.

- *Amber*: Attracts prosperity and wealth; known as a natural aphrodisiac for both sexes; nullifies obstacles and negative vibrations.

- *Apple*: Brings good luck and protects you from enemies.

- *Azahar*: Provides happiness, joy, and renewed energy; helps combat work-related stress; use to dissipate concerns.

- *Azucena (lily)*: Attracts peace and quiet; use to channel energies and entities of higher planes.

- *Balm*: Fights witchcraft and keeps away evil spirits.

- *Benzoin*: Purifies and protects against evil; use to cancel various spells.

- *Bergamot*: Combats stress and depression; use to raise self-esteem.

- *Camphor*: Dispels all kinds of negative energies when burned; use to ward off bad influences and repel enemies, and to develop clairvoyance.

- *Cannabis*: Stimulates psychic energy, clairvoyance, meditation, astral projection, and contact with other worlds.

- *Carnation*: Attracts love, protection, and good luck; also has aphrodisiac properties.

- *Cedar*: Disperses and exorcizes evil; purifies old or uninhabited places and attracts prosperity.

- *Cherry*: Attracts love, happiness, and abundance.

- *Cinnamon*: Cleanses enclosed spaces from all types of negativity; protects against envy and the Evil Eye; use as an aphrodisiac.

- *Citronella*: Conjures good luck; ideal for outdoor use because it repels mosquitoes.

- *Clove*: Channels monetary energy, money, wealth, and abundance.

- *Coconut*: Stimulates wisdom and understanding; strengthens clairvoyance and divination during sessions conducted in private; use in rituals as an aphrodisiac.

- *Copal*: Dissipates negative energies and entities; also widely used in divination and meditation.

- *Eucalyptus*: Protects against evil spirits sent to harm and disrupt; strengthens concentration and dispels anxiety and vices.

- *Forest*: Channels the energies of Mother Earth and attracts the spirits of Nature for healing rituals or as protectors.

- *Frankincense (Olibanum)*: Attracts good energy and peace; most recommended incense for meditation; fights panic attacks and anxiety.

- *Gardenia*: Attracts love and passion.

- *Geranium*: Provides calm, tranquility, and confidence; use to consecrate all kinds of amulets and talismans.

- *Ginseng*: Stimulates and energizes; use to ward off envy and bad vibes in the workplace.

- *Honeysuckle*: Facilitates divination and all rituals that put you in direct contact with the spiritual plane.

- *Jasmine*: Attracts inspiration, good luck, wealth, and fortune; ideal for rituals linked to wealth and prosperity.

- **Lavender**: Cleanses the environment against "astral larvae" and all kinds of negative entities; unlocks the psyche and stimulates clairvoyance.

- **Lemon**: Attracts joy; stimulates positive thoughts and the development of dreams; dispels all kinds of energies, vibrations, and negative entities.

- **Lilac**: Attracts peace, calm, and love; also purifies corners impregnated with negative energy.

- **Lotus**: Keeps away negative influences and people; helps attract abundance, spiritual calm, and tranquility.

- **Magnolia**: Promotes health and mental agility; encourages development of the psyche, clairvoyance, intuition, and understanding; also prevents accidents.

- **Mint**: Supports concentration and keeps you focused on your target.

- **Musk**: Attracts prosperity and positive vibrations to the home; use as a powerful aphrodisiac; purifies against evil thoughts.

- **Myrrh**: Attracts peace and serenity; stimulates the development of clairvoyance; strengthens all kinds of spells and rituals.

- **Nard**: Promotes development of clairvoyance and psychic powers; protects against psychic and astral attacks.

- **Neroli (orange blossom)**: Heals and protects; also helps channel the energies of a beloved.

- **Nutmeg**: Renews energy and protects against disease.

- **Opium**: Attracts peace of mind and psychic protection; strengthens bonds in relationships and protects against third-party intervention.

- **Orange**: Promotes spiritual enlightenment, peace, and joy; also attracts money.

- **Patchouli**: Stimulates tired minds and protects against evil in general; widely used in rituals and spells associated with love, tranquility, and money.

- **Peach**: Brings joy and auspicious conditions; helps contact and call the beyond.

- **Pine**: Strengthens lost faith and encourages spiritual ties to ancestors; also protects against envy and jealousy.

- **Queen of the Night**: Attracts love and passion; powers rituals performed on Friday night, because of its relationship with Venus; used by women as an aphrodisiac.

- **Rose**: Stimulates positive dreams and attracts happiness, love, and joy; protects loved ones from misfortune and bad omens.

- **Rosemary**: Brings good luck and money; use to protect your home and its inhabitants against all kinds of negative entities, spirits, and spells.

- **Rue**: Enables the psyche and intuition; attracts good luck and prosperity; cleanses karma and attracts good omens.

- **Salvia**: Attracts material and spiritual prosperity; strengthens the mind and promotes inner calm.

- **Sandalwood**: Attracts success and material wealth; powers clairvoyance and spiritual development; use to embue charm bags with positive energies, as well as to facilitate meditation and astral projection.

- **Strawberry**: Attracts money, wealth, love, and prosperity.

- **Tangerine**: Attracts good luck, money, prosperity, and material wealth.

- **Thyme**: Wards off nightmares, fears, and panic attacks; protects against witchcraft and betrayals.

- **Vanilla**: Attracts love; strengthens the psyche; promotes sensuality and sexual desire.

- **Verbena (vervain)**: Protects against all evil; use to clean and purify all kinds of environments; attracts prosperity and stimulates the desire to learn.

- **Vetiver**: Strengthens rituals and amulets tied to money and material wealth.

- **Violet**: Attracts love and elegance; combats envy and promotes mental and spiritual healing.

- **Ylang ylang**: Channels energies that promote love, passion, sensuality, and sexual desire; aphrodisiac.

Attributes and Their Incenses

- **Aphrodisiac**: amber, coconut, musk, vanilla

- **Attract good luck**: amber, jasmine, mandarin, sandalwood

- **Attract love**: cherry, carnation, strawberry, ylang ylang

- **Combat insomnia**: orange blossom, geranium, lavender, thyme

- **Combat stress**: geranium, lavender, mint, orange blossom

- *Enhance concentration*: eucalyptus, mint, rue, sage
- *Fight depression*: bergamot, frankincense, jasmine, patchouli
- *Improve health*: apple, ginseng, neroli, nutmeg
- *Meditation*: azucena, copal, lotus, tuberose
- *Protection*: lemon, myrrh, rosemary, sandalwood
- *Purification*: camphor balm, eucalyptus, lemon

Zodiac Signs and Associated Incenses

Fire Signs
Aries

- *Daytime*: cinnamon, honeysuckle, rose
- *Nighttime*: honeysuckle, lavender, verbena (vervain)

Leo

- *Daytime*: cinnamon, frankincense, rue
- *Nighttime*: amber, clove, frankincense

Sagittarius

- *Daytime*: cinnamon, orchid, sage
- *Nighttime*: cedar, patchouli, sage

Earth Signs
Taurus

- *Daytime*: clove, lily, sandalwood
- *Nighttime*: clove, ginger, mint

Virgo

- *Daytime*: lavender, lilac, sandalwood
- *Nighttime*: jasmine, lavender, orange blossom

Capricorn

- *Daytime*: lily, sandalwood, vanilla
- *Nighttime*: gardenia, pine, vanilla

Air Signs
Gemini

- *Daytime*: carnation, mint, musk
- *Nighttime*: mint, orange blossom, vanilla

Libra

- *Daytime*: jasmine, musk, violet
- *Nighttime*: geranium, orange blossom, violet

Aquarius

- *Daytime*: aloe vera, musk, orange
- *Nighttime*: aloe vera, jasmine, magnolia

Water Signs
Cancer

- *Daytime*: geranium, magnolia, pink
- *Nighttime*: amber, geranium, lemon

Scorpio

- *Daytime*: eucalyptus, lotus, rose
- *Nighttime*: clove, lotus, tuberose

Pisces

- *Daytime*: lotus, magnolia, rose
- *Nighttime*: frankincense, lily, magnolia

Incenses by Day of the Week

Sunday

- *Daytime*: cinnamon, frankincense, rue
- *Nighttime*: almond, rue

Monday

- *Daytime*: amber, geranium, magnolia
- *Nighttime*: benzoin, geranium, jasmine

Tuesday

- *Daytime*: honeysuckle, lavender, lotus
- *Nighttime*: honeysuckle, myrrh, orange

Wednesday

- *Daytime*: lavender, musk, sandalwood
- *Nighttime*: copal, musk, sandalwood

Thursday

- **Daytime**: orchid, patchouli, sage
- **Nighttime**: cedar, neroli, patchouli

Friday

- **Daytime**: lilac, pink, violet
- **Nighttime**: jasmine, rose, ylang ylang

Saturday

- **Daytime**: gardenia, lily, vanilla
- **Nighttime**: copal, lily, verbena

Appendix E

Candle Magic

Candle magic is an essential art common to traditional witchcraft and white magic that you must learn in order for your magical rites and incantations to be effective. Candle magic is a basic tool of witchcraft and perhaps one of its most important components.

The colors of candles are tied to universal principles. Red candles symbolize love, while white candles mean purity and green ones represent money. Many studies have been done on the magic of colors to help us understand how each color affects us physically and emotionally, as well as on a spiritual and astral level. In Europe, for instance, mages traditionally wrote wishes in rhyme on paper and burned them in the flame of a silver candle on the night of the Full Moon so the Moon goddess would listen and grant their desires. Lighting a white candle every night brings you the protection and blessings of the spirits. Lighting a white candle on behalf of deceased relatives grants them rest and peace and gives them strength to continue on their way. A black candle eases the pains and fears planted by others; a gold candle provides you with the tools you need to fulfill your wishes. Magical practitioners use their knowledge of colors to perform all kinds of spells and rituals and when they craft charm bags, amulets, and talismans.

In magic and sorcery performed with candles, all the basic principles of magic come into play: intention, breathing, and visualization. Articulate your goal clearly and focus your intention on it. Breathe deeply several times and visualize your desires and goals manifesting. Then pray to the spirits or gods of your personal pantheon and light an appropriate-colored candle whose flame will consume the obstacles in your way and whose smoke will carry your desires to the astral plane to be heard by the higher entities.

Candles are a fundamental tool for all kinds of sorcery. They symbolize our ability to create and to dominate a situation. They are among the basic elements you must gather and prepare before you perform your rituals. By lighting a candle, you activate your magic power within its blessed flame. The power of the Fire element in the flame consumes your desires and cravings. The spell or ritual you perform strengthens those desires with your power and faith. And the smoke from the candle flame invokes the energies of the Air element to carry those messages to the Great Spirits so they can execute your wishes and grant your desires.

Candle Colors and Their Attributes

Here is a list of the different effects you can obtain using different colored candles.

- **Black**: The color of shadows and darkness. Black symbolizes nocturnal magic and all the creatures that inhabit the night. It is the color that results from the absence of all other colors and emotions. Psychological studies have shown that people who often dress in black want to go unnoticed. It is an unemotional, although very elegant, color—the color of loneliness, depression, and fatigue. Those who can not fight their own battles and those who fail to accept themselves wear this color. It is an absorbing, sad, and depressing color that you should avoid wearing except in situations that require it.

The Magical Art of Crafting Charm Bags

It symbolizes the thoughts we keep hidden—despair, disappointment, solemnity, lack of self-esteem, grief, and sadness. It is the color of suffering souls. Black has the ability to absorb all the energies around it.

- **Blue**: The color of sympathy, harmony, friendship, and trust. Rituals associated with eternity, fidelity, nobility, freedom, and independence usually include this color. It is the color of the seas and oceans, symbolizing freedom of thought and the arts. It opens the mind and brings peace and tranquility. Blue, in all its shades, has the power to override negative energies. It is associated with the immune system and helps calm fevers and aches. It has also been proven to help relax the mind and reduce stress. It is the perfect color for decorating student dorms and scientific laboratories. A person dressed in blue exudes a feeling of confidence and calm as well as independence.

- **Brown**: The color of the Earth and all its essential elements—sand, rock, and soil. Brown has some bitter attributes, but is also the color of seriousness, maturity, diplomacy, and good character. It is the color of collaboration and working people. It symbolizes the powers of the Earth to regenerate and heal all ills, as well as the healing powers of plants. It is associated with the spirits of the Earth element—gnomes who take care of the garden, fauns and nymphs, as well as higher spirits who protect forests and natural sites. A brown room promotes reliability and character and is the most appropriate color for an office. Wearing brown clothes gives you a presence anywhere and provides aspects of maturity. It is the color of merchants and businessmen.

- **Gold**: The color of the Sun god. We relate the color gold to material riches, wealth, pride, satisfaction, discoveries, and positive energy. It symbolizes beauty, happiness, luxury, and solemnity, and is the color of kings and emperors. Gold is related to the healing of emotional issues, personal satisfaction, and inner beauty. A gold room brings you the feeling that you have achieved your goals and are proud of your achievements. To wear gold garments symbolizes luxury and glory and attracts attention and positive energy. It helps you win the favor of the elves and makes your personality shine. But too much of it can give the wrong idea to others.

- **Green**: The color of health and hope. Green represents Mother Nature, Gaia, and all the spirits that inhabit the forest. It symbolizes balance, durability, fertility, life, and goodness, and attracts health, success, creativity, physical balance, and mental strength. It is the color of spring, fairies, and elves. It stimulates the intellect and the desire to improve. In its various shades, green brings healing. It is a hypnotic color—soothing and sedative—that has healing and protective properties. It also symbolizes fertility and strengthens endurance and renewal. A light-green room encourages ingenious ideas and calm. It is the right color for young boys entering puberty, as it gives them mental calm and stimulates neuronal development. Dark green is recommended only for common areas like hallways and gardens because it has an intense and energizing tone. Do not wear yellowish-green clothing because this is the color of disease and can cause negative moods. Pale green tones bring calm and healing to those around you.

- **Indigo**: A powerful color for the psyche. Indigo has both sedative and stimulant properties. It is related to the brain and its functioning, and is associated with ambiguity, synesthesia, intuition, and extrasensory perception. It is also the color of children with special needs. Indigo is a mystic, deep, and mysterious color that promotes the development of individual faculties and strengthens intuition and powers of telepathy. It also has protective and soothing qualities. In candle magic, use indigo for all spells related to mental development, curing various parts of the brain, and understanding or studying something new. It is the mystical color *par excellence* and is used in rituals to protect children and seniors.

- *Orange*: The color of joy, positive energy, and dynamism. Orange stimulates creativity and intelligence, as well as good taste and sociability. It is a unique color, as it does not exist in the astral plane. It is only visible on this plane, and only to the living—the dead can not differentiate orange from simple yellow. Orange is an energetic, charismatic, and abundant color with positive vibrations. It symbolizes performance and positive mood changes and gives you an extra dose of energy. It is a healthy color that stimulates you mentally and emotionally. It is an incandescent color—fiery, sensual, vibrant, and upbeat—the right color for promoting teamwork, communication, personal security, and self-confidence. It is an excellent color to wear on days of celebration or days when you feel listless and tired. An orange room helps you wake up every morning with energetic vibrations, but staying in an orange room too long can become irritating and stressful.

- *Pink*: The color of love and romance. Pink symbolizes femininity, illusion, dreams, eroticism, vanity, delicacy, and charm. It is the color of love, of family, and of eternal friends. It produces a feeling of affection and emotional sensitivity and is also the color of devotion and innocence. Combining the qualities of red and white—vitality and purification—it balances skill and finesse. Pink, or rose, is the classic color of romanticism. A room with an abundance of pink promotes long and stimulating conversation, affection, attachment, romance, and lasting friendships. It is the best color for the bedrooms of girls when they enter puberty because it discourages irritability, indifference, and mood swings. Pink clothing gives a humble, quiet, and submissive appearance, although it can also give its wearer a unique quality to cope with and adapt to all kinds of groups and situations.

- **Purple, violet, mulberry**: These are the colors of positive change, transformation, and transmutation. They also have the power to raise the spirit to different levels and develop powers of extrasensory perception. Purple has powers of transformation and transmutation, spiritual elevation, and mental development. It is the color of the ancient gods and can reverse any situation to your advantage. For students or practitioners of metaphysics, this is the color that transmutes energies and thoughts. It can turn any situation, however difficult it may seem, into a positive situation for you. Violet shares the powers of blue and red, though to a lesser extent than either one individually. It is the color for transforming situations related to justice and feelings and is widely used in witchcraft to search for objects and missing persons. It symbolizes devotion and faith, vanity, magic, and access to the spiritual world. Mulberry, like violet, shares the properties of blue and red, but also has the power to open portals to the spirit world. It is the most visible color on the astral plane and can alter the personality.

- **Red**: The color of fire, love, passion, dreams, life energy, and blood. Red represents vitality, sensuality, and good health, and protects you against envy and negativity. It is also the color of hate, aggression, danger, desire, strength, and stamina. It is linked to heart and blood magic, and is one of the primary colors that has the power to alter feelings. Red is full of energy and vitality. Its use should be limited to small areas of the home to bring life and good memories. In clothing, it is only suitable for certain occasions because it promotes sexuality, vigor, and lust for power. It should be used sparingly because it tends to cause eyestrain or excessive fatigue, and can sometimes promote aggressiveness and anger.

- **Silver**: The color of elemental metals. Silver symbolizes good position, promotions, elegance, and respect for old age. It is the color of warriors and anyone working with metal and is the color of the Moon goddess. Next to white, it is the color best suited for protective spells and rituals, and can strengthen all kinds of charms performed at night under a visible Moon. It is the color of invocation. Silver is a color full of character. It has its own personality but also functions to reflect other forces and attributes. It is a good companion for all dark colors and gives you presence. It is an elegant color that gives you wisdom and intuition to make decisions. It protects you from external influences and is the color of the seers—providing stability, generosity, and independence. On the other hand, unlike silver, gray is an opaque color without character that should be avoided because it can make you dependent, bored, and easy to influence.

- **White**: The color of spirituality, calm, peace, tranquility, thought, wisdom, and understanding. White is the color associated with all that is ethereal and intangible, and also symbolizes purity, meditation, and spiritual strength. It is the color of great sages and is commonly used in magic to purify places or people and to cleanse the aura. White is related to faith and clarity—a purifying color that, for centuries, has been considered the color of the beyond and of major life changes. White rooms promote calm, tranquility, and peace. In excess, it can cause boredom and feelings of loneliness. Wearing white allows you to think with clarity and purify the atmosphere around you. It projects an image of calm and peace to those around you. It is the color to wear when attending funerals and charity events because of its quality of emotional cleansing and because it symbolizes the tranquility of the spiritual.

- **Yellow**: The color of joy, happiness, and good humor. Yellow is the color of sunshine and flowers that attract wealth. It symbolizes pleasure, fun, friendliness, and optimism, as well as greed, selfishness, and jealousy. People with yellow auras are usually happy, intuitive, and very curious, as well as highly intellectual and rational. But they need someone to push them continually to achieve their goals. Yellow is associated with the digestive system. It stimulates hearing, the nervous system, and creativity, and is the color of dreamers. A yellow room usually gives a feeling of warmth and comfort, although, in excess, it can alter you. Wearing yellow attracts energy and good humor and gives you a positive image in front of others.

Rituals with Colored Candles

Here are some brief rituals and spells that call on the energies of different colors that you can try at home to get experience before going on to more elaborate magic. Each ritual involves lighting a candle of a specific color to demonstrate how the use of the right color can be essential to getting your intended effect. In most of the rituals, the candle is moistened first with an appropriate incense. This is called "dressing" the candle. Remember that the colors of the candles given are not interchangeable and play an important part in guiding the magic toward your desired effect.

- **Black**: Black is the color of depression, melancholy, and Gothic culture. Black candles actually can override sadness, however, and help you get out of a depression or help you end your grief. Just apply a few drops of rosemary oil to a black candle and light it between dusk and midnight.

- **Blue**: Blue candles are used to empower your magic and strengthen you. Use this easy ritual to boost your power. Dress a blue candle with mixed essential oils of lavender and amber. Light your dressed candle at noon.

- **Brown**: Brown is the color of dirt, wood, and earth. A brown candle can help you guide the Nature energies toward healing effects. Anoint a large brown candle with a few drops of myrrh oil and light it after sunset. Use this to strengthen any healing ritual.

- **Gold**: Gold is the color of the Sun—the ruling star that gives life to the Earth and its inhabitants. To win the favor of the Sun, use gold candles—always an odd number of them. You can light them at dawn, noon, and sunset. You can also perfume them with natural oils of jasmine, sandalwood, and even lavender.

- **Green**: Green is the color of dollar bills, so it seems logical to use it in rites to attract money. You may think that paper money is a recent invention and that gold is more traditionally associated with wealth, but gold candles have a much more profound use. If you just want to help your economic situation or even to improve your working conditions, light a green candle. First, mix essential oils of cedar and gardenia, then use them to dress a green candle. Light the candle in the evening, and you will feel how things start to get better.

- **Orange**: Orange candles can work to boost your self-esteem and restore your physical energy. Anoint an orange candle with essential oils of sage and orange and light the dressed candle in the morning. You will realize what a wonderful person you are.

- **_Pink_**: Pink candles can be used for protection for you and your loved ones. People tend to underestimate the power of this color. In the morning, light a pink candle previously dressed with a mixture of camphor and rose oils. You can also use bergamot oil.

- **_Red_**: Red is the color of passion and love. If you need more love in your life, just use more red candles. Rub a red candle with a mixture of essential oils of pepper and roses, light the dressed candle at dusk and feel the love that night.

- **_Silver_**: The Moon goddess is sometimes called the Silver Mother because silver is her color. If you want to gain the favor and blessing of the Moon, offer her silver candles. Light them in your window or on a balcony on the first night of the month that has a visible Moon. You can also dress the candles with pine or musk oils.

- **_Violet_**: Violet can transmute negative energy into positive energy. If you want to do so, or if you feel a place's energy and vibrations are out of balance, dress a violet candle with a few drops of essential oil of amber and light it at midnight—the witching hour—to have the best effect.

- **_White_**: White candles are used in most rituals along with colored candles, but they are crucial when doing a protection spell or a spiritual cleansing. This simple ritual is specifically made for both effects. Dress a large white candle with essential oils of both lavender and jasmine. Light the dressed candle on the night of the Full Moon and feel the purity.

- **_Yellow_**: Yellow is the color of friendship, so yellow candles are vital when looking for friends. To attract and renew friendships, dress a large yellow candle with a mixture of essential oils of cedar and sage. Light the dressed candle in the morning and you will be surprised how easy it becomes to make friends.

Index of Charm Bags, Amulets, and Rituals

About the Author

Elhoim Leafar, a resident of New York City, is a shaman, diviner, and traditional magician who hails from a family of spiritual and magical practitioners from Venezuela. He is also a palm reader and dowser dedicated to teaching the principles of practical magic and spirituality. Visit him at *www.elhoimleafar.com*.

To Our Readers

Weiser Books, an imprint of Red Wheel/Weiser, publishes books across the entire spectrum of occult, esoteric, speculative, and New Age subjects. Our mission is to publish quality books that will make a difference in people's lives without advocating any one particular path or field of study. We value the integrity, originality, and depth of knowledge of our authors.

Our readers are our most important resource, and we appreciate your input, suggestions, and ideas about what you would like to see published.

Visit our website at *www.redwheelweiser.com* to learn about our upcoming books and free downloads, and be sure to go to *www.redwheelweiser.com/newsletter* to sign up for newsletters and exclusive offers.

You can also contact us at *info@rwwbooks.com* or at
Red Wheel/Weiser, LLC
65 Parker Street, Suite 7
Newburyport, MA 01950